"I hadn't meant to read *My Vertical Neighborhood* in a single sitting, but Lynda's warmth, authenticity, and vision made me realize I was encountering a soul-friend—which is what I suspect happened to her neighbors, who we meet in this book. Anna and Ron, Yolanda and Nicolai, Brian and Rachel could not be more different, but they become Lynda's found family—and, through this book, ours. Her beautifully told stories made me long for the kind of community she describes. Friendships filled with awkwardness and acceptance, feasts and forgiveness, trust and tenderness. Lynda doesn't offer a how-to on hospitality. There's an industry that already supplies that. What she offers is something far more important. She resets our imagination through tales of lost parrots and Christmas pajama parties. A tender dance in a nightclub and a fast friendship formed at a Starbucks. Unexpected prayer requests from Kiribati and unanswered spiritual longings in a Bible study. Studies tell us we live in the loneliest era in history. Lynda invites us into a better story."

Greg Jao, senior assistant to the president, director of executive office communications and external relations, InterVarsity Christian Fellowship/USA

"Riveting, fascinating, authentic, vulnerable, funny—this book grabbed me and I could not put it down. Lynda's neighbors are established, lonely, secular urbanites in a high-rise apartment building. When she prioritizes them over church connections, they become her best friends. What does it mean to love a neighbor? 'Pay attention,' she says. 'Notice. Engage. Welcome. Open your door. Accept their invitations. Give time. Laugh. Debate. Apologize. Forgive. Cry. Celebrate.' Caught up in the quirky lives of Brian and Rachel and Yolanda, we see how community can flower in sterile spaces, and urban hangouts can be sanctified. There is awkwardness and misunderstanding and swearing and sex talk and even invitations to strip clubs, but the joy of Jesus shines through."

Miriam Adeney, associate professor of world Christian studies at Seattle Pacific University, author of *Kingdom Without Borders: The Untold Story of Global Christianity*

"The storytelling in *My Vertical Neighborhood* is both masterful and mesmerizing as Lynda MacGibbon captures heartwarming, humorous, and often vulnerable moments on her journey to meeting, loving, and learning to be loved by her neighbors. In this book, MacGibbon dares us to dive deeper into developing bona fide friendships with neighbors whose lived experiences might differ from our own."

Eric Lige, music director of the Ethnos Global Network and Urbana conference worship director

"Whether you live in a tall apartment building or a tiny house on a quiet street, *My Vertical Neighborhood* will make you want to throw your doors open wide and invite the neighbors in. This beautifully written chronicle of risk taking, hospitality, success, and even the sadness and struggles of building community for the sake of loving neighbors well over the long run, is inspiring and also practical. There are good ideas in these pages. After reading it, I want to shop for salty olives and some really good bread, and throw a dinner party for my neighbors."

Karen Stiller, author of *The Minister's Wife: A Memoir of Faith, Doubt, Friendship, Loneliness, Forgiveness, and More*

"In this intimate introduction to living intentionally into a community, Lynda MacGibbon captures the inconvenience and surprise of what happens when you take the call to live deeply into the world where God has placed you. Your neighbors become your friends, your friends become your community, and then the discoveries begin. Lynda has lived this out, fully and generously. She shares this intimate journey with us in *My Vertical Neighborhood*, and we are better for it."

Gary and Carla Nelson, former president of Tyndale University and author of *Leading in DisOrienting Times* (Gary), and research professor at Tyndale University and the Africa liaison and education specialist for Canadian Baptist Ministries (Carla)

"This heartwarming story is told with honesty and humor as Lynda introduces us to some of her friends. Spending time in her vertical neighborhood helps us see our own place with fresh eyes. Many of our lives are marked by transience and business. Despite living in close proximity to many, we often struggle to have any quality relationships. In our modern, busy world, how do we respond to Jesus' call to love our neighbor? Lynda's story is about her journey to deepen relationships, build friendships, and share faith in a new and challenging environment. She writes with an earthy realism that helps us think and makes us smile. This is not a how-to book, but it is encouraging, inspiring, and a little bit wonderful. It shows that it is possible to love our neighbor in a fragmented world and to build community one friendship at a time."

Nigel D. Pollock, president of InterVarsity Canada

"If you have ever been curious about how to connect the love of God with the love of our actual neighbors, you should read this enchanting book. Lynda MacGibbon's winsome storytelling invites us into the journey of mutual transformation that so many of us are longing to experience. Better yet, she gently shows how these sacred opportunities are literally all around us."

Tim Soerens, author of *Everywhere You Look: Discovering the Church Right Where You Are*

Lynda MacGibbon

My VERTICAL *Neighborhood*

How Strangers Became a Community

Foreword by Michael Frost

ivp

An imprint of InterVarsity Press
Downers Grove, Illinois

InterVarsity Press
P.O. Box 1400, Downers Grove, IL 60515-1426
ivpress.com
email@ivpress.com

InterVarsity Press® is the book-publishing division of InterVarsity Christian Fellowship/USA®, a movement of students and faculty active on campus at hundreds of universities, colleges, and schools of nursing in the United States of America, and a member movement of the International Fellowship of Evangelical Students. For information about local and regional activities, visit intervarsity.org.

All Scripture quotations, unless otherwise indicated, are taken from The Holy Bible, New International Version®, NIV®. Copyright © 1973, 1978, 1984, 2011 by Biblica, Inc.™ Used by permission of Zondervan. All rights reserved worldwide. www.zondervan.com. The "NIV" and "New International Version" are trademarks registered in the United States Patent and Trademark Office by Biblica, Inc.™

While any stories in this book are true, some names and identifying information may have been changed to protect the privacy of individuals.

The publisher cannot verify the accuracy or functionality of website URLs used in this book beyond the date of publication.

Cover design and image composite: David Fassett
Interior design: Daniel van Loon
Images: textured background: © R.Tsubin / Moment Collection / Getty Images
group eating: © courtneyk / iStock / Getty Images Plus
elevator button panel: © Wicki58 / iStock / Getty Images Plus
high rise apartment building: © B.S.P.I. / Corbis Documentary / Getty Images

ISBN 978-0-8308-4740-2 (print)
ISBN 978-0-8308-4792-1 (digital)

Printed in the United States of America ♾

InterVarsity Press is committed to ecological stewardship and to the conservation of natural resources in all our operations. This book was printed using sustainably sourced paper.

Library of Congress Cataloging-in-Publication Data
A catalog record for this book is available from the Library of Congress.

P *25 24 23 22 21 20 19 18 17 16 15 14 13 12 11 10 9 8 7 6 5 4 3 2 1*
Y *42 41 40 39 38 37 36 35 34 33 32 31 30 29 28 27 26 25 24 23 22 21*

FOR MY NEIGHBORS.

Thank you for trusting me to tell this story.

Contents

Foreword

Michael Frost

*I*n *My Vertical Neighborhood*, Lynda MacGibbon tells the story of leaving her charming three-bedroom Cape Cod house with a knotty crab apple tree and a towering poplar in the quiet town of Moncton, New Brunswick, to move into the hustle and bustle of high-rise living in Canada's largest city, Toronto. It sounds like *Green Acres* in reverse. Remember that whimsical show about a Park Avenue couple relocating to a dilapidated farm in Hooterville only to discover a charming sense of community among the quirky locals? It's a story played out in movies such as *Sweet Home Alabama*, *Doc Hollywood*, and *Hope Floats*.

However, depictions of rural people moving to the city are rarely so cheery.

When filmmakers imagined urban life in the twenty-first century, it was as far from *Green Acres* as you could picture. From Fritz Lang's *Metropolis* to *Back to the Future* and *Blade Runner*, the city was often depicted as a dark, wet, Orwellian dystopia of high-density living, soaring buildings, and freeways (and, of course, flying cars). Moreover, in other films about country folk forced to relocate to the city, the urban landscape is depicted as an unsafe zone where people feel anonymous, uprooted from their usual support structures, and disconnected from the rhythms of the seasons and the traditions of family or clan.

We love stories about city folk moving to the country and reconnecting with people and the earth and being drawn back into life. But we don't think life is found in the city, much less in urban high-rise developments. Philosopher Zygmunt Bauman described the individual lost in the hubbub of urban life as

> a pilgrim without a destination; a nomad without an itinerary . . . [who] journeys through unstructured space; like a wanderer in the desert, who only knows of such trails as are marked with his (*sic*) own footprints, and blown off again by the wind the moment he passes the vagabond structures the site he happens to occupy at the moment, only to dismantle the structure again as he leaves.[1]

He's describing a sense of never-quite-belonging; that feeling where you owe the community nothing and they owe you nothing in return; where your roots don't go down very deep into the soil; where you can relocate at the drop of a hat because all apartments are alike and all neighborhoods are roughly the same. They are nomadic and never-placed. They try to smile through it all and say things about how they can bloom wherever they're planted, but the only plants that can do that are grown in a soulless factory greenhouse.

After over two hundred years, you'd think we'd be better at addressing the impact of industrialization and urbanization on traditional beliefs and structures and human well-being, but as Ann Morisy puts it, "We are living in troubled times and people have become bothered and bewildered. And when people become bothered and bewildered, great caution is needed because our instinctive response is scapegoating and death-dealing."[2]

Since Morisy wrote that, the world has been hit by the cata-
clysmic effects of climate change and the stultifying consequences
of a global pandemic. People are bothered and bewildered, alright.

Little wonder that in American cities such as Minneapolis, Fer-
guson, Baltimore, and Oakland, peaceful protests against racism
and police brutality have recently erupted into riots, looting, and
arson. Urban living can foster a sense of alienation and rage anyway,
but when you throw in social need, discrimination, and racism,
people explode. And the authorities respond in the only way they
know how—with riot gear, tear gas, sound cannons, police dogs,
concussion grenades, rubber bullets, pepper balls, wooden bullets,
beanbag rounds, Tasers, pepper spray, and armored vehicles.

Of course, with the collapse of the rural sector, people pour into
our large population centers looking for work and educational opportunities, for better healthcare options, and for the perceived
tolerance of alternate and diverse lifestyles.

However, none of that explains why Lynda MacGibbon moved
into her Toronto apartment.

She felt *called*.

If city dwellers are indeed bothered and bewildered, easily given
to scapegoating and death-dealing, we need people like Lynda,
who are willing to leave their Cape Cod homes and move into
high-rise buildings to embody the love of God in that place.

I have a friend who defines the church as "Christians in the
neighborhood who are joining in God's dreams for that place," and
that's what Lynda describes in this book. We know God's dream
for a neighborhood does not include social isolation, disconnection
from the earth, racial division, poverty, and fear. Scripture reveals
that God's dream is for a beautiful redeemed world, filled with
justice, where human beings are reconciled to God and with each
other, where sickness, disease, violence, and greed are no more. This
means that God's people are to move into neighborhoods (both

physically and relationally) and partner with their neighbors in seeing this dream take form.

In his book *Everywhere You Look*, Tim Soerens commends Christians to not only care about their neighbors, but also to seek the shalom of everyone and everything in their neighborhood. In so doing, he believes they form the connective tissue that brings hope and healing to our divided society. But, interestingly, he says such a project will not be completed by those with a "savior complex" who wade into neighborhoods with promises to fix and heal everyone. No, Soerens says, it begins by *listening*. By being truly present, attentive, and inquisitive. Soerens quotes Peter Block telling a group of neighborhood leaders, "Don't be helpful, be curious."[3]

As you read Lynda MacGibbons's book you will encounter a genuinely curious person. You'll observe her interactions with the recently separated Rachel, and the unfolding collaboration that ensues. You'll meet Fran and Brian and Yolanda and many others, and you'll watch as their lives intertwine and as loneliness and fear fall away.

Lynda MacGibbon might have moved into her apartment building in order to help or serve her neighbors, but what she describes is the beautiful work of allowing neighbors to find and help each other. In this vortex of collaboration, friendship, and kindness, God's dream unfolds inexorably, endlessly, toward the intended end.

My Vertical Neighborhood is not so much a manual on how to be an urban missionary as it is a gentle, inspiring memoir about neighborliness itself, and the way God works through us when we submit to the practices of humility, presence, and otherliness.

Fran from the Eleventh Floor

*Y*ou're new to the building," Fran observed, giving me a welcoming smile as I stepped into the elevator. She didn't bother to extend her hand, seeing I was clearly in no position to reciprocate. "What floor?"

"Fifteen. Thanks so much," I answered gratefully as she pressed the button and the elevator began moving upward.

My arms were full—one elbow was wrapped around an overgrown potted fern, while my hand clutched a three-legged table. I'd slung a bag over my other shoulder, stuffing it with a blanket, a table lamp, and a couple of small pots and pans and had pressed a framed watercolor of tulips against my side. Like most high-rise dwellers, I was becoming adept at carrying as much as possible from the underground parking lot up to my apartment. Unload in one trip. That was the rule everyone seemed to live by, even if it meant we were constantly dropping things along the way.

"I moved in a few months ago," I said, then gesturing down at my full arms, "I'm still getting settled."

"I'm Fran from the eleventh floor. If you need anything at all, come and find me."

"Thanks so much. I'm Lynda. It's so nice to meet you."

Then the door opened, and with a wave, she was gone.

A moment later, I was in my own apartment, setting the plant on the kitchen counter and propping the picture against a wall. I dropped my bag of odds and ends on the floor and surveyed the mostly empty room. A recently purchased couch was pushed up against floor-to-ceiling windows, and two lawn chairs and a folding table occupied another corner.

Placing the fern on the small table, I crossed the room and set them down next to the couch. Then I returned to the kitchen, untangled the blanket from the pots and pans, and carried it to the couch, draping it across the cushions. Standing back, I surveyed the room again.

"That's better," I said out loud. I'd been living in the near-empty apartment for several months, most of my furniture two thousand miles away in a house I'd not yet been able to sell. I didn't want to empty the house too soon, thinking people were more likely to buy it if they could imagine themselves sitting on an actual couch, eating breakfast at an actual table. When it finally came time to drive my car across the country, I'd packed it with only a few necessities—the pots and pans—and as many treasures as I could fit. The plant, the picture, and the blanket were small but helpful comforts, familiar objects that made me feel a little bit more at home in a city I was hoping would one day actually be that. Home.

My thoughts went back to Fran, how friendly she'd been. *Would I have the courage to take her up on her offer of help? And even if I did, how would I find her?* She hadn't given me her phone or apartment number.

"Fran from the eleventh floor," I mused. "Will I ever see you again?"

Chasing a Question

*T*he year before my fiftieth birthday, I upended my life. Sometimes when I'm feeling a bit stuck, I rearrange the furniture or cut my hair. But there have been a few times in my life when I've needed more than a room makeover or a good stylist to loosen whatever it is that is constraining me. When that happens, I recognize the need for upheaval, the kind that requires a moving truck.

When I was forty-nine, I said a nervous but hopeful yes to a new job, one that meant relocating from my small city in eastern Canada to Toronto, the fourth largest city in North America.

Moncton, New Brunswick, where I'd lived for twenty-two years, has a population of about 140,000 and one high-rise (with twenty floors). Toronto is home to more than 9.2 million people, many of them living in the city's more than two thousand high-rises (some towering sixty-five stories into the sky).

The size of the city was daunting enough, but Toronto also had a reputation, and it wasn't good: "Toronto thinks it's the center of the universe. Toronto drivers are crazy and the commutes unbearable. It's unaffordable. Unwelcoming. No one wants to live there unless they have to. And no one can buy a house. It's too expensive."

But I said yes. When the offer came, I already knew I'd been looking for a change—I just hadn't been anticipating one quite so big. I'd become too comfortable and was feeling restless. More often than not, I was having conversations with myself that went something like this: "Is this it? I love my house. I have wonderful friends and a cat that loves me as unconditionally as a cat can. My work is meaningful, and my mom and sister's family live a three-hour drive away. I am most at home in the rugged, open landscape of Canada's east coast. But is this enough?"

At the time, I could not have fully explained why life as I knew it was not enough. I sensed it had something to do with how neat and predictable my life had become. How it felt small, confined. I had good friends, a purposeful job, and a church where I was so involved, I had my own key.

But I'd recently spent four summers living in Almaty, a Central Asian city about as different from Moncton as I could ever have imagined. Surprisingly, I'd felt at home among the 1.2 million people who lived there. I was intrigued by its diversity—Kazaks, Koreans, Uzbeks, and Germans are just four of its 120 people groups. I discovered I loved the complexity of a big city, the warrens of apartment complexes, and the way people lived their lives in public parks rather than private backyards.

When I moved to Moncton and purchased my first house, I told my real estate agent he'd never make more money from me, since I planned to live there well into my retirement. At the time, it was exactly what I wanted—a one hundred-year-old farm-house in a part of the city that felt more rural than urban. The house was quirky with uneven floors and a stone foundation so porous crickets and mice came and went at their pleasure. In the living room, seven windows filled the space with light by day; a fireplace warmed the room at night. The kitchen, with its bay window and wicker rocking chairs, was the heartbeat of many parties. There were three bedrooms upstairs: one for me and two for my frequent guests.

The house was graced with ancient lilac and honeysuckle bushes, grape vines, birch trees, and a knotty crab apple tree that provided so much fruit neighbors helped themselves without asking. A massive Carolina Poplar towered above the house and yard, a sentry I saluted each time I drove across the bridge that spanned the river below my house. That tree, high on the hill where my house stood, was a stalwart friend, always assuring my home was in sight, no matter where I'd come from or how long I'd been away.

I gave it all up—my three-bedroom Cape Cod house and generous yard—for exactly what Toronto's reputation had suggested I'd get: a 900-square-foot apartment with a decent view but a kitchen far too small to provide life support for any party. I went from living close to the land to living high in the sky, fifteen floors off the ground. Fortunately, I wasn't afraid of heights.

I exchanged the Carolina Poplar for Lake Ontario, a far less stable sentry, but still a satisfying presence. I traded seventeen flowerbeds for a stretch of public parkland, hedged—to my delight—by swaths of untamed lilacs. I did not give up my love of gardening. Instead, I cultivated it to fit my new space, experimenting by planting purple coneflowers and daisies, along with chives, thyme, and rosemary. Every spring I watched to see what shoots would emerge from my small pots of earth, hoping some plants had survived winter on the balcony. As the season warmed, I planted Tiny Tim tomatoes, hot peppers, sugar snap peas, and carrots that were sweet but short in stature. Not everything was adept at growing so far off the ground. Rhubarb, which pretty much thrives anywhere, did not appreciate the confinement of my balcony garden. I was particularly frustrated by this discovery because in Moncton I'd been blessed with two sprawling rhubarb patches planted long before I'd ever acquired the property.

Over time, I became happier in my new home than I'd initially expected. My apartment faced Lake Ontario, and I could see

Toronto's skyline to the east and the faint plumes of Niagara Falls to the southwest. Sunrises were stunning, rays of red and gold spilling across the lake and filling my living room with light. Sunsets reflected off the towers in downtown Toronto, transforming the city center into a collection of glittering jewel boxes.

Who lives in all those boxes? I wondered as I gazed out my windows at the distant towers. And, who, for that matter, lives next door to me, in the half-dozen high-rises in my new neighborhood? Would I ever meet the people who lived so close we could exchange a cup of coffee across balcony railings? I wanted to meet them. I just didn't know how to make it happen.

It didn't help that the transition from one place to another had proved more difficult and disorienting than I'd expected. I accepted the new job in April, but my employer asked me to continue doing work in New Brunswick until the end of the year. For nine months, I traveled back and forth between Toronto and Moncton, and friends there started asking me why I was still around—hadn't I moved already? In Toronto, my relationships were limited to work colleagues and my brother's family who lived in a nearby town. I appreciated their anchoring stability, but I held back from relying on them entirely.

I did this on purpose. I suppose you could say I'd decided to engage in a social experiment, although I was more likely to describe it as wrestling with a theological conundrum, one that had been nagging me for a while.

Why did God command me to love my neighbor? What does this kind of love look like? What would happen if I tried to follow the command daily, not just when some random stranger seemed in need of my assistance?

I'd been pondering these questions for nearly a decade, ever since I'd heard a lecture by the Australian writer Michael Frost. He told a story of moving into a neighborhood with a few other followers of Jesus precisely so they could live out what Jesus says is the second-greatest commandment of all, the one that summed up the ten given to Moses on Mount Sinai and the hundreds of others written in the Hebrew Torah. It's the commandment Jesus references in three of the four Gospel books of the Bible when asked what he considered to be the first and greatest commandment.

"Love the Lord your God with all your heart and with all your soul and with all your mind and with all your strength," said Jesus (Mark 12:30). But he didn't stop there. He added: "The second is this: 'Love your neighbor as yourself.' There is no commandment greater than these" (Mark 12:31).

I've spent a lot of time in my life learning to love God with my heart, soul, mind, and strength. I was raised in the kind of Christian family that considered church an extension of our home life. I work for a nonprofit organization that helps young people discover Jesus and follow God for a lifetime. Back in my own university days, I was one of the students they helped, and much of my learning about loving God has come from surrounding myself with other believers who are both thoughtful and practical about their faith. And while there were lots of people in my life—classmates, extended family, coworkers—who did not share or approach faith as I did, the biggest investment of my time was reserved for those who were committed believers like me. As an adult, whenever I moved to a new town or city, I looked for friendship and community first among people who, like me, went to church more often than not and devoted at least one evening a week to a small-group Bible study.

That didn't leave much room for anyone else.

Specifically, it meant I didn't have much time for my neighbors, for the people I might encounter who did not share my beliefs about God or any of my other values either. Until I heard Frost speak, I wasn't even aware I was putting so much effort into loving

God that I'd missed the other half of the great commandment, the part about loving our neighbors. I knew it was a commandment, but I'd equated it with all the other commandments in Scripture. Jesus doesn't do that. Jesus says loving God, self, and neighbor is foundational to everything else. If we don't understand and practice these conjoined commandments, it will be harder to obey the rest.

Long before moving to Toronto, I'd figured out who my neighbor might be—anyone in my sightline. The Good Samaritan is in one of Jesus' most famous stories, and even people who don't know the details are often aware of what the phrase means: to honor, care about, help, and respect someone who is a stranger, who is nothing like you, who might even be considered an enemy but is still worthy of your consideration.

But what it meant to love such a person was a mystery to me. Like, enjoy, appreciate, welcome, tolerate, respect—these words all made sense when it came to interacting with neighbors. But love? How would that work its way into my relationship with people I bumped up against, especially the ones who lived nearby, but weren't family, fellow churchgoers, or lifelong friends?

It wasn't that my parents didn't believe in this particular teaching—they were gracious in their hospitality. Years after they moved away from the neighborhood of my childhood where they'd lived for forty-two years, they were still in touch with friends who shared our street, calling to wish them happy birthday, sending cards and flowers to mark deaths, making a point of sharing a meal when they returned for a visit. But, perhaps because church life took so much of our time, I grew up separating the world into two groups—those who were devout Christians and those who were not. Most of our close friends came from the former category, and while there were exceptions, they were few.

I doubt my parents intended for me to adopt the perspective that love was mostly reserved for fellow Christians. In fact, they taught us that all people deserved our neighborliness—our kindness, politeness, and hospitality. I liked and appreciated people who didn't share my beliefs and rarely shied away from friendships that came my way. But it never really occurred to me to approach each person I encountered with a default inclination of love. That particular teaching of Jesus was lost to me.

Michael Frost made me helpfully uncomfortable, and his story attached itself to me like a small burr.

Frost seemed to set his clock by both neighborly and liturgical time. On Sunday mornings, he would often head to the ball field where families were hanging out with their kids. When an artist in his neighborhood expressed hopes for an upcoming show, Frost and his friends offered to design posters and cater the event—at no cost. Bible studies in his home attracted not only his Christian friends, but a diverse collection of neighbors as well, many of whom had never read Scripture. As I listened to him speak, I could tell Frost loved his neighbors and they loved him back. I was inspired as I listened to him talk.

And so, when I moved to Toronto, I made a conscious decision not to follow what had been my practice for the first forty-nine years of my life. I would not look for new friends primarily among my Christian colleagues. I wouldn't expect my brother's family to provide for my relational needs. I would be careful about how much time I spent at church.

When, after six months of searching, I settled into a church in my neighborhood, I met with the pastor, Jim, for the usual get-acquainted visit. Somewhat apologetically, I explained I wouldn't be there every Sunday because I was trying to leave space in my life for my neighbors, and Sunday mornings seemed to be when they were available. Tamping down my guilt, I said I wouldn't be available to serve on committees or sing in the choir or help with youth group or teach Sunday school: all the things I'd readily done in previous churches.

To my relief, Pastor Jim responded with enthusiasm, blessed my decision, and asked me to let him know how he and the church could pray for me and the people who lived around me. When I did show up at church, he always asked me how things were going in a way that I knew he meant it.

Even with Pastor Jim's prayers, meeting my new neighbors proved more difficult than I'd expected. I tried lots of things: I joined the condo gardening committee, brought meatballs to the annual Christmas potluck, and went to every business meeting in the building, smiling at whoever sat next to me. I said polite hellos to people in the elevator and even had a few extended conversations in the hallway with the woman who lived two doors from me.

But the conversations never went beyond a superficial hello, how are you, hope you have a good day. It helped if someone had a dog—then you could ask the dog's name, admire the color of its fur, inquire about its age. Somehow it was appropriate to ask questions about dogs; less so their humans. I rarely asked people on the elevator to share their names, but I always asked what they called their pets.

We were an arm's length away from each other, the hundreds of humans (and almost as many dogs) who made up my vertical neighborhood. We were stacked on top of and squished alongside each other, so close you would think it impossible not to become acquainted with one another. But it was. Walk along any hallway in my building and you'd see door after door, each looking exactly like the other. Walk by those doors often enough and eventually you'd stop seeing them, let alone give a passing thought to the people living on the other side.

In his book, *Incarnate,* Michael Frost encourages people to not only follow Jesus and obey God's commandments but to be like Jesus and to live fully into them.

An incarnational posture, writes Frost, requires that we move into neighborhoods. Be attentive, listen to the people around you.

Stay with people for a long time. He quotes the writer Wendell Berry: "Love your neighbors, not the neighbors you pick out but the ones you have."[1]

Frost helped me rethink my understanding of my neighbor. But I didn't want to just think about it, I wanted to live it. Faith as a belief system alone has never satisfied me. I resonated with Frost's words: "An inner conviction is only worthwhile to the degree it is embodied in action."[2]

I wanted to live differently. I prayed a lot. Pastor Jim prayed. My conviction grew, but my actions seemed to keep hitting a wall. All those doors along the hallways of my apartment building remained closed to me. And then Rachel moved in, and everything began to change.

3

Two Are Better than One

*R*achel and I met by divine appointment. Sure, the meeting was in a predictable place: a Toronto Starbucks. And, true, it was actually set up by a human, someone keen on connecting us because I had a job opening at work that I desperately needed to fill, and Rachel was desperately in need of a job. It was a what-do-either-of-us have-to-lose kind of meeting, the goal of which was mutual relief. But here's the divine part: the threads we offered each other that day were eventually spun into a tapestry of friendships woven in the most unlikely of places—my Toronto neighborhood. On the day we met, neither of us imagined that might happen.

It was December, just a few days past Christmas. The weather was frigid, and the streets were like ice rinks. They weren't un-navigable, but they definitely demanded we pay attention to where we placed our feet. I think about it now as much more than a wintery walk. For both of us, that day marked the beginning of a longer journey that hasn't always been easy but has been well worth the effort.

I arrived at the coffee shop ahead of Rachel, ordered my usual decaf skinny vanilla latté, and claimed the only remaining table in the middle of the room, a couple of feet to the left of the counter.

It wasn't ideal, but not much in my life was at that time, so I was grateful we at least had a place to sit.

I was wearing hiking boots to better navigate the ice, and blue jeans to better fit in with a group of university students I'd met that morning. The students were attending a conference hosted by my organization in a nearby church. In my role as communications director, I'd spent the morning taking photographs and interviewing third- and fourth-year university students about what they were hoping to do with their lives. Technically, I was on Christmas vacation, but I had no one else to send to the conference, so I'd squeezed it into my already full day. Earlier that morning, I'd packed a suitcase and cleaned out my fridge.

When it came to life experience, I was years ahead of those students; I knew what I needed to do to put the pieces together in a way that made sense. A couple of hours after my meeting with Rachel, I was scheduled to fly back to Moncton so I could oversee the moving company I'd booked to pack up my house. I had finally sold it, which meant I could turn the page on the next chapter.

Rachel strode into Starbucks promptly at 1 p.m. wearing four-inch stilettos, a slim black skirt, and a pink blazer. *How on earth,* I wondered, *had she climbed the snowbanks? And wasn't she cold?*

Her makeup was impeccable: blue-grey shadow dusting her eyelids, black eyeliner framing hazel eyes, a touch of color on her cheeks. She extended her hand toward me as she sat down, placing a black portfolio on the table between us, her posture straight and movements precise.

"Hi, I'm Rachel. I'm so glad to meet you." She had a big smile, her scarlet lipstick dramatic against straight white teeth. She did not look like a woman whose life, as I happened to already know, was in turmoil. But then, external appearances aren't everything—on that day, dressed in jeans and a fleece sweater, nothing but a wisp of rouge on my own cheeks, I didn't look much like the communications director for a twenty-million-dollar nonprofit organization.

"Thanks so much for coming to meet me," I replied. "Let me buy you a coffee. What will you have?"

"Whatever is the darkest roast," she replied. "But you don't have to pay for it." I waved away her objection as I stood up and turned toward the counter.

Rachel's taste in coffee, I eventually discovered, was like her taste for life—enthusiastic and bold. Over the years of our friendship, while I've acquired a taste for many of her preferences, coffee has never made the list.

Rachel had come to Toronto from Wisconsin to spend Christmas with her mother and adopted aunties—four women who had lived together for thirty years and who worked for the same organization as me. It might have been the festive season, but life was not all goodwill and cheer for her. A few months earlier, she had discovered her husband of seven years was having an affair.

Her marriage over, Rachel was exhausted and heartbroken. And she needed a job.

My boss had discovered Rachel's graphic design experience over dinner at the aunties' house the night before and had called me to suggest Rachel and I meet.

Years ago (I don't remember exactly when) someone (I don't recall who) told a story that I've never forgotten. The story was about watching silk rugs being woven in a Middle Eastern market. As weavers sat on the back side of the fabric, steadily weaving their threads back and forth, a master weaver walked back and forth on the front side, observing the emerging pattern. Sometimes the weavers' hands produced flawless patterns; sometimes they made mistakes. The master weaver never asked the weavers to undo the mistakes; instead he subtly changed the pattern, incorporating even the mistakes into the overall design.

I have carried that story with me ever since as a metaphor for the life I live as a follower of Jesus, a believer in God. The story of my life is not mine to weave alone. There is a master weaver at work. Nor am I the only one contributing to the design of my life—others will add their threads, whether I want them to or not. There will be missed stitches, faulty threads; some will break and fray. But there will also be true and intricate ones, rich colors, even gold. As I look back on my life, I see the way it's been threaded together with far more complexity than I'd ever be able to accomplish by myself. I've experienced this enough to believe it's true.

That day in December, although Rachel and I didn't fully realize it, we were threading our lives together. We both thought our meeting was about work—about me needing a graphic designer and her needing a job. But it turned out to be about much more than that. As we sat sipping our coffees in the middle of that crowded Starbucks, our lives were becoming more than we'd ever dreamed or imagined.

Looking back on it now, I can see the clues were there. About fifteen minutes in, the interview morphed into a heart-to-heart conversation as we talked about recent changes in our lives—her separation, my relocation—and about our work philosophies. We discovered we both valued collaboration and neither of us was afraid to start small and build toward something bigger, especially if we were doing it as part of a team.

By the time two hours had passed, we also realized we liked each other.

"Would you move to Toronto?" I asked Rachel, not quite sure how we'd obtain a working visa for her. I'd already interviewed half-a-dozen out-of-work candidates. Unemployed graphic designers weren't exactly in short supply in Canada.

Rachel allowed a long pause to settle around us. I kept silent. And then, "Yes. I'd move to Toronto."

"Then let's pursue this," I said.

Much to our surprise, trade agreements between Canada and the United States included certain jobs cleared for easy work visas, and graphic designers were on that list. Rachel arrived in March, moving in with her mom and aunties until she could figure out where she wanted to live in the city.

In August, I asked Rachel to look after my apartment while I was on vacation. I figured it would be mutually helpful—she could water my balcony garden while taking a break from life in a houseful of women. She loved her mom and aunties dearly, but Rachel was thirty-four and had not lived with her mother for many years. I thought I was doing Rachel a favor when I offered her my two-bedroom, two-balcony apartment for a few days of respite. I knew she was an early riser—my sunrise view over Lake Ontario would be one gift, the chance for solitude another.

I misjudged. She hated it.

When her marriage ended, Rachel gave up a sprawling house with a veranda and several acres of land in rural Wisconsin. Life in a concrete and glass tower was not what she imagined for herself. It was not restful; it only reminded her of everything she'd lost.

Ultimately, it didn't matter. She called me one evening, interrupting my vacation. When I asked her how things were going, she told me she hated high-rise living. Then she surprised me by saying she was considering renting an apartment, not just in my building, but on my floor. Would I mind, she asked, if in addition to working side by side, we lived that way too?

I was ecstatic. *But how,* I wanted to know, *had she gone from despising high-rise life to deciding to make it her home?*

While I'd been away, Rachel had started looking at apartments, sensing it was time to move out of her mother and aunties' house and into her own space. Contrary to her usual thorough research tactics, she'd viewed exactly two apartments. The first was a spacious second-story walk-up above a bar in a down-at-the-heels neighborhood. If she had to live in a city, this was the kind of street she favored. The second option was a four hundred-square-foot, one-bedroom apartment overlooking a six-lane expressway, with no view of the lake or the sunrise.

"I don't know why," she said, "but the moment I walked into that small condo, I felt like I was at home. It has nothing that I want in an apartment." She paused and then asked, "Would you mind if I lived on the same floor as you? After all, we work together every day. You might not want me around after work as well."

"When are you moving in?" I replied. "I can't wait!"

I meant it. Her decision was the answer to a prayer I'd been sending up to God ever since I'd moved to Toronto. Rachel, I was certain, would make it easier for me to meet my neighbors.

4

A Little Bit of Crazy

*W*hy haven't you just invited people in?" Rachel asked me one Saturday morning in September, not long after she'd moved into the building. We were sitting on my balcony, the sunshine warm on our faces. I'd set out bowls of strawberries and grapes, a platter of scones, and a chunk of aged Gouda on the round glass table between us. Rachel had carried a pot of her own coffee down the hall, not trusting what I might brew. We each drank our own coffee that day, a pattern that has continued through our friendship. Most things we agree on; a few, not so much.

We settled in for a long conversation. Neither of us had anywhere else to be; in fact, we'd purposely reserved the day so we could talk about what we each hoped might come from sharing life in our neighborhood.

"As a single person, it seems odd to invite people I don't really know into my place," I said in answer to her question. "I guess I'm nervous. What if they say no? What if they're crazy and I can't get them to leave?"

Rachel took her time replying, as if she was waiting for her thoughts to arrange themselves into sentences before approving their release. She looked out over the lake, the view split in half by the condo tower directly in front of us. To the right, far down on the ground, tiny construction workers milled about in a cavernous hole, pouring concrete and moving steel to lay the foundation for yet another high-rise. The sounds of their work crashed against our peaceful Saturday morning. On Saturdays, they worked until noon and then vacated the neighborhood until 7 a.m. on Monday morning, when their digging and hauling and drilling and hammering would begin again. Our neighborhood was a perpetual construction zone in those days, the clamor of clanging metal filling the air, fine particles of concrete constantly layering dust on couches, floors, beds, and every other available surface.

"It's nearly impossible for me not to meet people," Rachel finally responded. "Whether it's in the elevator, a coffee shop, at the concierge desk. Everywhere I look, there are people. Some people love reading books—well, people are like books to me, inhabiting worlds that are different than mine. Each person I meet gives me a different perspective on life. I want to know about their worlds."

I opened my mouth to respond, but Rachel held up her hand. "Wait, I'm not finished with my thought." Over the years of our friendship as I waited for her often long, drawn-out thoughts to resolve and present themselves, I learned to listen, to keep my mouth shut for just a little longer than had been my habit.

"I probably have a little bit of crazy in me," Rachel finally said. She tucked her muscular legs up against her chest, rested her bare feet on the edge of the chair, and wrapped her arms around her knees. I wished I could sit like that, but resigned myself to propping my short, fat legs on a nearby flowerpot, buttering a scone as I continued to listen.

"For me, the risk is worth it," she said. "Inviting someone into my life doesn't feel particularly risky. I'm not afraid of people knowing who I am—my faith, my habits. I don't keep my circles tight." She paused, then continued: "There is a real question of safety. You don't know who the person is, if they're going to stalk you. I've had weird moments. But I've felt God protecting me. Sometimes I think I may have put myself in compromising situations and miraculously survived!"

As Rachel talked, I looked out on the building in front of me, at its empty balconies, closed curtains. *Where were all the people? What occupied their Saturday mornings?*

I shifted my gaze downward to the trails that wound through the park by the lake. I could see people walking and biking, pushing strollers, and tossing balls for their dogs. Some walked hand in hand, couples, obviously together. Some were in small clusters, friends, families out in the sunshine. But many were solitary.

I didn't fully realize it then, but Rachel's little bit of crazy was exactly what I needed to free myself from the fear of inviting strangers into my life. I wanted more than polite, fleeting conversations in the elevator or hallway. I wanted to welcome neighbors to cross the threshold of my home, to sit on my couch and stay, maybe not quite until they decided it was time to leave, but at least long enough for a genuine conversation.

"So, where do we go from here?" I asked Rachel.

"Well," she replied. "I think we should pray. I think we should ask God what we should do next."

Prayer would become a regular part of the conversations Rachel and I shared. Sometimes the idea to pray tumbled out of a conversation like the one on my balcony that morning, an obvious next step as we considered how to meet our neighbors. Sometimes we set aside particular times for prayer, both sensing that involving God would make things go better. God was, after all, the one who first came up with the idea about neighborly love.

As summer drifted into fall, Rachel and I met once a week at a nearby coffee shop to pray together. As the autumn chill tickled our necks, we'd sit at an outside table, coats pulled tight, praying out loud with our eyes open, as if we were simply in conversation with each other. We figured we'd draw less attention that way—not that Rachel was concerned about it, but I was.

By the end of October, we'd made two decisions about next steps.

One involved food. The other, stories. Both proved necessary ingredients for meeting—and more importantly, learning to love— our neighbors.

5

Opening My Door

*I*n late November, Rachel and I decided to throw a party. We placed invitations against the sixteen apartment doors on our floor, listing our own names and apartment numbers and suggesting people bring food and drinks to share. We were banking on people accepting an invitation if it came from two neighbors instead of one. My apartment was larger than Rachel's so it made sense for me to host, and, with her partnership, I felt more confident about inviting a group of strangers into my home.

On the night of the party, I propped open my door and slid two homemade chicken and pesto pizzas into my oven, hoping the scent of garlic and basil would entice people who might be having second thoughts about joining us.

I needn't have worried. Nine neighbors came through my door that evening, everyone bringing something to contribute. The retired couple living across the hall from Rachel brought a red bean and rice casserole, treating us all to a taste of their home country of Colombia. A single guy with Jamaican roots contributed a six-pack of beer, promising his mother's jerk chicken for the next party. The woman whose apartment was kitty-corner to mine arrived with a vegetable platter, then slipped out midevening to retrieve lemon squares still warm from her oven. Two other women whose apartments were on either side of the elevators set bottles of wine on the kitchen counter as they made their way into the living room. A Chinese couple from down the hall brought pastries for dessert.

We sat in a big circle, five people on the large, corner couch I'd purchased for this very purpose when I moved to Toronto—I wanted people to sit comfortably in my home, even though it was small. Others sat on chairs pulled away from my drop leaf dining table, more useful for holding drinks than to provide eating space for so many people. We balanced our plates on our laps, an arrangement that would become the norm, even when I was eating dinner all by myself.

We ate and drank, sharing stories of moving in, of how long we'd lived in the building, and why we'd chosen this particular part of Toronto. The conversation was pleasant and, when people finally left the party, they offered a common parting line: "Thanks. I've always wanted to meet my neighbors."

Tidying up the kitchen after everyone had left, I was pleased with myself. Pleased that I'd invited my neighbors in and that we'd all learned a little about each other. Pleased that it had all been so respectful, so enjoyable.

The next morning, sitting alone on my couch, feet resting on the wooden blanket box that served as my coffee table, I wrote about the evening in my journal, effusive about how successful it had been:

Last night, I discovered something more about what Jesus meant when he said love your neighbor as yourself. When you love your neighbors, you invite them into your life—into your home. You eat, talk, laugh together. You ask questions about who they are, their families, you enjoy their company. Love God and love your neighbor as yourself. That's a profound commandment. The world would be so much better if we all followed it.

I thought I was well underway in my quest to understanding what it meant to love my neighbors. In reality, I had barely cracked open the door. I had taken notice of my neighbors. I'd even invited them into my home and had spent a pleasant few hours with them, offering hospitality and welcome. These were worthwhile actions and they made us all more aware of one another. But it took me a while, and a few messier gatherings, to realize that we'd barely begun to explore neighborly love that night.

A more honest way to describe what I was practicing that night is what Scot McKnight calls "safe neighbor love."[1] In his book, *The Jesus Creed*, McKnight encourages followers of Jesus to replace the word *safe* with *sacred*—to view others with reverence, with utmost value. "Loving others means that we seek to restore humans to God and to one another. We all fall short, so we need to ask: What can we do? What can we do to restore humans to one another? To make things right? We can look, we can see and we can act."[2]

Most of the polite people who crossed the threshold of my apartment that night remained on the periphery of my life, even though we continued to live along the same hallway, even though we could (mostly) remember each other's names. In the months and years to come, I learned it would take much more than one polite gathering for me to grasp what it truly meant to love my neighbors and, perhaps as importantly, to accept their love for me.

It would take, among other things, eating together every week, not once a year during the Christmas season. And ultimately, it would require more than food and drink, although those ingredients were important.

At the floor party, Rachel made an announcement: beginning the first week of January, she would be opening her door every Monday night for dinner. Anyone interested in food and company was welcome to stop by between 7 p.m. and 9 p.m.

On the first Monday, the two women who lived nearest the elevator, and were within sight of Rachel's open door, showed up. The next week, and the week after that, there was no one—just Rachel and me, working together all day and then, as the evening set in, trying not to talk about the tasks we'd left behind at the office.

"Maybe this isn't going to work," I said on the third Monday as we sat across from each other, Rachel in the swivel rocker she'd rescued from an estate sale, me on the 1950's leather settee that once furnished a doctor's office. Rachel loved vintage furniture for its appearance more than its comfort.

We were tearing slices from a loaf of crusty bread, spreading it with butter and triple crème Brie as we talked. Five steps across the room, in a galley kitchen that was tinier than mine, chicken stew simmered in a crockpot. As usual, Rachel had made enough food for a dozen people or more.

She looked down at the glass in her hand, swirling it slowly, then looked at me. "It's going to take consistency. We have to be here week after week so people understand this is not just a one-off thing."

"You're probably right," I said. "I'm also realizing it's going to take commitment. It means that this is what I do on Monday evenings, whether it's just you and me or not. Good thing you're an excellent cook."

Rachel stood up and placed her glass next to the row of white and turquoise boxes lining the shelves on one wall of her apartment. In addition to 1950s furniture, she appreciated efficient design.

"That's true," she laughed. "I am a good cook. Would you like a pinch of cilantro in your stew?"

Eventually, more people began to make their way through Rachel's doorway on Monday nights. Curiously, hardly any of them were our fifteenth floor neighbors. Mostly, they were people who'd randomly met Rachel somewhere in the neighborhood—in our building's hot tub, at the bus stop, or at the coffee shop around the corner. Wherever she met people, Rachel always invited them to Monday night dinner.

Rachel and I were born fifteen years apart and on opposite sides of North America—she on the coast of the Pacific Ocean in California, me on the coast of the Atlantic Ocean in Newfoundland. Her parents divorced when she was thirteen; mine were together for more than forty years until my dad died from a heart attack.

Although their marriages ended differently, all four of our parents embodied a value for hospitality, which they'd bequeathed to us, their youngest daughters. We both grew up in generous homes where guests were frequently at the dinner table, dropping by for tea, or staying the night in a spare room. Rachel and I came by hospitality naturally, but we worked it out quite differently. She grew up in free-spirited California where life was mostly lived in the limitless outdoors. I grew up in Newfoundland where seasons create their own boundaries and the people follow suit. Rachel extended hospitality on a whim, inviting strangers home without a second thought. I was cautious, usually needing an introduction before I opened my door to someone new.

My invitations were far less frequent and more measured. One of the first people I invited was Elizabeth, a single woman in her twenties who lived two doors from me. During the first year of our acquaintance, Elizabeth and I never made it past her doorway or mine, although we had plenty of conversations. Often, as I was making my way down the hallway at the end of a day's work, I'd find Elizabeth putting the key in her door. Unlike some hallway greetings, Elizabeth's always seemed to include a secondary question that invited more conversation.

"How was your day?" she'd ask. Or, "Did you hear about the new entry gates management is installing on the building?" Elizabeth, a healthcare consultant who worked from home, was a deep source of information about things going on in our building. Sometimes we'd end up chatting for twenty minutes, grocery bags dropped at our feet, coats still on.

Then one evening, the power went out. It was the first outage I'd experienced since moving to Toronto, and I knew exactly where to go to find out what had caused it.

"What's going on?" I texted Elizabeth.

She replied instantly. "Some massive outage—the whole block is out. Hydro One says it will be a few hours before it's back on."

"Hmm," I texted back. "There's a lot of police cars and fire engines in the building across the street. Wonder what that's all about?"

"Ooh, that's interesting! I'll see what I can find out," came the quick reply.

We texted back and forth for about ten minutes, until finally I wrote: "You should just come over. You can watch the excitement on the street from here."

"I'm in my pajamas," Elizabeth texted back.

"Me too," I replied.

A few minutes later, Elizabeth and I were sitting across from each other on my couch, our faces lit by flickering candles and our phone screens (Elizabeth was still sleuthing). We talked long into that night, the semidarkness opening up more space for real conversation than our well-lit but narrow hallway ever had. By the time the power came back on, we knew our hallway visits had come to an end. From then on we took our conversations beyond our doorways and into each other's lives.

The next Monday, Elizabeth showed up for dinner at Rachel's, becoming one of the regulars, although she never ate. Elizabeth was on a mission to get her body in shape and kept her food choices tightly controlled. By the time I met her she was training for her first half marathon. Often on Monday nights, we'd see Elizabeth twice—first a brief check in and then for a longer visit.

"Hi, I'll be back—I'm just going home to clean up," she'd say, poking her head around the corner of Rachel's open door, her thick red hair tied back with a bandana, sweat still glistening on her forehead. "Don't wait for me—I'm not eating! But I'll be back." Fifteen minutes later, she'd return, eager to report on how many minutes she'd shaved off her run that evening.

Once she began joining us on Monday evenings, Elizabeth also started extending our invitation to people she knew in the building. One woman was skeptical.

"No," Elizabeth assured her, "there's no hidden agenda, just friendship."

When Elizabeth relayed the conversation to me, I wondered if she was right. Was it just friendship Rachel and I wanted to offer people? We were both followers of Jesus and he expressly says we should tell others about him. Was that what we were really about?

The answer was complicated. I'd set out to meet my neighbors because that's what the religious creed I follow instructs me to do. I wanted to find out why that tenet is so fundamental to Christianity, why Jesus says loving God and neighbor makes everything else fall into place. But I'd also been schooled in all the other teachings of Jesus, including some of the last words he spoke on this earth: "Go into all the world and preach the gospel" (Mark 16:15).

I pondered the question one morning in my journal and on that day, at least, seemed at peace with my own motivation:

We do want people to experience good, true, welcoming friendship. And I do want people to know that Jesus is at the heart of everything Rachel and I do. But I can honestly say I have no other agenda than to love God and love my neighbor.

It was too early in my Toronto life to actually understand what that meant, although I probably thought I knew at the time. I still had so much to learn. And I still hadn't even met most of the people who would help teach me.

Much to my delight, one of those people turned out to be Fran. Fran from the eleventh floor. Fran, the friendly neighbor I'd met in the elevator shortly after I moved in. When Elizabeth invited her to dinner, she readily accepted, not concerned at all about whatever motives were behind our hospitality.

Fran became a Monday night regular, usually wandering into Rachel's apartment an hour after most people, a cut-glass tumbler of gin and tonic already in hand. Always stylish, she favored tunic-styled sweaters over leather pants that flattered her slim legs. A black-and-silver choker or chunky necklace added sparkle and she'd applied her makeup as if she was going out to a fancy res-taurant. Fran was a beautiful, fifty-something-year-old woman whose smile sparkled even more than her jewelry.

"I should cook for all of you some night," Fran frequently offered, then quickly added, "But I've kind of given up on cooking. I haven't entertained for years. Still, maybe I should give it a try again."

Rachel's weekly invitation was never contingent on reciprocity. No conditions propped open her door and no reservations were necessary for a seat in her living room. She had no expectation that guests would bring food or beverages, although people fre-quently did. She rarely had to buy wine or sparkling water for Monday nights.

Rachel cooked dinner nearly every Monday night for five years. On the odd Monday she was away, I cooked and people filled my apartment. Every now and then, one of our neighbors would offer to host. But mostly it was Rachel preparing enough food for a banquet, even though on most nights only four or five people showed up. Having more than enough was a hallmark of her hos-pitality. Sometimes more than a dozen people crowded in, perching on her vintage chairs, the benches she kept stored beneath her shelves, and the bar stools at her kitchen counter. When necessary, people sat on the floor. No one complained.

Rarely, after those first few lonely weeks, was it just the two of us sitting looking hopefully at her open door. She was right about consistency, and I was right about commitment. Throw those two ingredients into dinner plans, and guests will come.

Over the years, conversations grew deeper and more profound as we ate together on Monday evenings. It became easier to be silly with each other, and we laughed a lot. Nothing was off topic—ours was not the sort of gathering that had rules against talking politics, religion, or weight loss programs. Rachel and I only had one rule— everyone was welcome. Sometimes the conversations became uncomfortable and someone would stop coming, sometimes for a few weeks, sometimes forever. But over the five years, a core group of neighbors remained, and there were always new people coming and going.

Commitment and consistency, an abundance of food and drink, an open door, and plenty of prayer. All of these things helped transform a group of strangers into a community. Eating together every week was important, but it would take more than that to help me figure out the answer to my theological question. Getting to know my neighbors was one thing—loving them proved to be something else entirely, especially when Brian entered my life.

6

Unfurling Our Stories

*R*achel met Brian a month before I did. Conversation bubbled up between them in our building's hot tub, where both were seeking respite from sports injuries. As they soaked their sore muscles, they chatted on and on. By the time they stepped out of the water an hour later, Brian had invited Rachel to a Sunday morning breakfast in his apartment, and she had said an immediate yes.

I thought she was crazy. "What if he's a serial killer?" I demanded. "You can't go to some strange guy's apartment without knowing anything about him!"

But she wasn't afraid, explaining it to me this way: at one point during the course of their hot-tub conversation, Brian held his hands out toward Rachel, palms open and flat.

"You know," he had said, "in this world I just want to live my life openly. You get into a relationship and you think it's like this, but then you do something and it bothers somebody and a wall goes up like this." Rachel watched as Brian snapped his palms together.

"All of a sudden," he went on, "you're living in this tiny place where you can't live openly at all. You're completely constrained by other people's expectations and values. Wouldn't it be great if someone just received us like this?" Brian opened his palms wide again.

"How," Rachel asked me, "can I not go to breakfast with someone who talks like that?"

I knew better than to argue. But I made her promise to text me before and after the visit so I could at least pray she'd come out alive.

After that breakfast, Brian and Rachel's friendship deepened rapidly: dinner at our neighborhood Italian restaurant, an evening glass of wine and conversation in her living room, bike rides along the paths by the lake. She'd tell me each time they were connecting, but more than a month passed before she introduced him to me, which I found perplexing at the time.

From the very beginning of their friendship, Rachel and Brian were transparent with each other, talking openly about their divorces, deepest fears, and most regrettable mistakes, but also how much they loved dancing, the risks they were willing to take in relationship, their views about God. They were alike in their candid approach to conversation. If someone asked them a question, they'd give an honest answer.

I thought I knew how to be transparent, too, until I began spending time with Rachel and then Brian. Their frank disclosures shocked me into realizing how little I actually ever said about myself, how little I thought there was to say. I'd worked as a journalist for a big chunk of my life, and I was more accustomed to asking questions than answering them.

Besides, my life up until that point seemed almost dull compared to the people I was meeting in my new neighborhood. I'd rarely dated and had never been married or divorced, never had children. I came from a fairly intact family, and had more than enough friends all over Canada and around the world to suit what I thought were my needs for relationship. I was content with my life, optimistic, and sometimes too cheerful for Rachel's liking.

"Don't you ever swear?" she'd asked me early in our friendship. "Don't you ever get pissed off?"

"Once in a while, but no, not very often," I replied. "Other than grade ten, when I cursed like a sailor everywhere except in front of my parents, I've never been one for swearing. Words matter to me, and I just don't like the sound of swear words much."

Rachel and I shared lots of conversations through the years about the merits of swearing, and she was especially delighted when I told her about a study I'd heard about—apparently avid swearing was an indication of intelligence and honesty.

"Maybe I should take it up in my old age," I joked.

In the early months of our friendship, I sensed Rachel's wariness about introducing me to people she was meeting outside of our Monday night dinners. She told me all about Brian, but she kept him to herself until the right time and place presented itself: the inaugural meeting of Writers' Group.

When Rachel and I brainstormed about inviting our neighbors into our lives we'd debated all sorts of ideas: a book club, weekly dinners, movie nights in the building's theater room. And then, one day, the idea of a writers' group emerged.

It came from Rachel, birthed in her mind for two reasons, one practical and one profound. I was the practical reason. I was a writer by trade, earning my stripes over the course of twenty-five years as a newspaper reporter and editor, teaching journalism and contributing to magazines and books.

"You can help people who want to write learn to do it better," Rachel said, adding, "and I think writing stories will help us get to know each other more quickly than through a book club where people mostly will just talk about the book. If we start a writers' group, people will end up writing—and then talking—about themselves. That will be way more interesting."

So, we set a date, put up posters in the mailroom, and agreed to bring plenty of food and lots to drink. Our building had a public dining room, so we booked it, thinking a neutral space would attract more people.

And so, there we were at 7 p.m. sharp on that first night, hoping that others from the building would join us in sharing life through the words we would set down on paper.

We set out bottles of red and white wine, Perrier, and soda next to the dozen wine glasses Rachel had carried from her apartment. We filled the table with platters of bread and cheese and bowls of hummus, olives, and grapes. The welcoming feast was meant to settle nerves: ours and those of anyone else brave enough to show up.

Beyond the glazed doors, we glimpsed a steady stream of people passing by on their way from the lobby to the elevators and their apartments on the floors above us. Beyond the window at the far end of the narrow room, streetlights sliced through the bleak winter's night, exposing empty flowerbeds and concrete sidewalks.

"Do you think anyone else is going to show up?" I asked Rachel as I set a bottle of chardonnay next to the merlot she'd already uncorked and was pouring into two wine glasses.

She pushed a glass toward me, lifted her own toward the ceiling and said, "Cheers. Here's to a new adventure!"

I picked up my glass, tapped it gently against hers, and blessed her words.

"Yes, here's to whatever happens tonight. At least we've started."

"I'm pretty sure Brian is coming," she said. "He's excited about this. Did I tell you he's already writing a book about his life?" She continued to arrange plates, napkins, and cutlery on the table. "So, at least there should be three of us."

Everything ready, Rachel and I sat down across from each other. "Maybe we should pray," she suggested, but before I could respond, the door swung open.

"Daaarling, I'm here!" a man with platinum blonde hair pushed his way into the room, his foot nudging the base of the door as he balanced a large tray holding two covered pots and a bottle of water. He set the tray down and extended his arms toward Rachel, who leaned into his embrace. Then they both turned toward me.

"Hi, I'm Brian," he said, reaching for my hand. "You must be Lynda. It's so great to finally meet you. Rachel, of course, has told me all about you, more than you probably would ever have wanted her to. She's probably done the same thing with you—told you more about me than you'd ever want to know. I'm really excited about this group."

"I'm glad to finally meet you," I said as I accepted Brian's hand, feeling the firmness of his grasp. He was handsome, tall, and fit. Wispy bangs slightly obscured his blue eyes, but his gaze was direct. He was wearing flip-flops, socks, and shorts. It might have been cold outside but, like most of us in the building, he knew the common spaces could be stifling.

Was he forty? Maybe fifty. I couldn't tell. But then, he probably had no idea of my age either. People often have mistaken me as younger than my fifty-plus years. I love them for their error and wish it were true.

"I cooked food," he said, lifting up lids and releasing the sweet and sour aroma of barbecued ribs and sauerkraut.

"So it's just the three of us, huh? Well, that's fine. Where do we start? You're the expert, right?" he said looking at me. "Rachel told me you were a writer. So teach us. I'm eager to learn about writing. I'm writing a book about my life. It's called *Chasing Rainbows*. This group is going to be perfect for me."

Brian's sentences were coming at me rapid fire, leaving me a little breathless. I was relieved when he finally sat down and began to eat, focusing all his attention on his food, shoveling it into his mouth the way he'd dished his words out a few seconds earlier. Brian, I would come to learn, rarely did anything in slow motion.

I don't remember much about the rest of our conversation that first night, except that we agreed we would choose one word, spend the next few weeks writing whatever came to mind, then gather again to read out loud what we'd written. There were few guidelines— people could choose to write fiction, nonfiction, poems, even a song lyric if they wanted. They could toss off one paragraph or labor over ten pages. We all agreed that critical feedback would be offered only if the writer asked. Otherwise, we'd simply listen and ask each other questions about what we'd heard.

"So what's our first word?" asked Brian.

"Neighborhood," I replied, having already thought about where a group like this might begin. "Let's write about the neighborhoods we lived in as children."

A nice, safe topic—that was my intention. After all, wouldn't that be the best, the most comfortable way for a group of strangers to write their way into each other's lives? Neighborhood. It seemed such a neutral word, not one stuffed with precarious meaning, in the way of some of the words we would eventually tackle.

Over the years Writers' Group met, we took our inspiration from single words such as *culture, currency, color,* and *change* and had fun turning objects such as *elevators* and *lunchboxes* and *bicycles* into stories. No topic was taboo (also one of our words). We wrote about *God* and *evil, fear* and *patriotism, love* and *divorce.* Sometimes our word choices—*sisters, ancestors, marginalized,* and, not surprisingly, *conflict*—brought painful memories to the surface that people bravely shared with the group. On some nights, we could only land on a word by tossing a dictionary's worth onto the table, finally choosing one because it was getting so late. *Rigidity, thirsty,* and *forgetfulness* came to us that way. And once, well into our Writers' Group life, we all wrote down phrases, placed them in a basket, and selected one. The random winner, *Pray to the owls, and see if they will listen,* produced magical results.

Before Writers' Group, I'd never fully realized how one word could open the door to such surprising places. I wasn't prepared for what could happen to a word when it was wrapped in vulnerability, anchored by honesty. After I'd been a part of Writers' Group for a few years, I began to appreciate that if you give even one word a little time and space, stories unfurl, fluttering around those who hear them, touching them, changing them. Month after month, I'd leave Writers' Group grateful for this truth, surprised by the places my own stories took me, chastened when I could sense my fellow writers knew I hadn't let the word take me far enough.

We didn't write that first night. Instead we sat around the table, emptying bottles, filling our plates, and talking about *why* we wanted to write. Just before we were ready to leave, another stranger stepped tentatively through the doors. Her name, she told us, was Tanya, and she had just started a condo Facebook group. She'd seen our poster and was hoping she might find contributors in a Writers' Group. We never fulfilled that wish, but Tanya became a regular. She rarely wrote, but always listened intently, slowly leaning ever closer into friendship.

Two weeks after the first meeting, the four of us gathered again in the dining room, sitting at what would become our regular seats: Brian at the head of the table, near the door, Tanya at the opposite end, Rachel and I across from each other so we could mentally telegraph prayers over the table. *God, please let everyone feel comfortable here. Let this be a safe place for our stories. Help us to really listen to each other.*

In case our prayers weren't fast-acting enough, we'd once again filled the table with platters of food and bottles of wine and Perrier. We settled in, scooping dollops of Rachel's homemade guacamole onto crisp tortilla chips. Brian passed around plates of spicy paprika chicken. He often worked from home and so had time to cook for us.

"I'll read first," Brian offered. "May as well get it over with." He pushed his plate to one side, lifted his black laptop off the floor, and placed it on the table. "God, I'm really nervous."

"Go ahead," Rachel said, looking at him. "I can't wait to hear what you've written. Can I read next, though? I might throw up if I have to wait too much longer. Is that okay with you?" She looked across the table at me. I couldn't tell if she was really nervous or just trying to make Brian feel better.

I felt relieved not to read first. Better to let everyone else read while attention spans were fresh, I thought, trying to convince myself that it didn't really matter what people thought of my writing. But I knew that wasn't true. I was as nervous as everyone else in the room.

Brian took a deep breath and cleared his throat a couple of times. Brushing strands of blonde hair away from his eyes, he began to read:

> It was the hunger that ensured that moment would rest forever in his long-term memory. They had arrived outside the apartment building with paper bags filled with groceries. Each of them were handed a banana, which they quickly devoured. They were also given a quarter, a fortune in those days. He would never forget that place. It was where she had taken them to escape their father, who apparently was an abusive husband. Now she was a single mother of three, living on welfare. He did not know what welfare was, but he knew it was a bad word, since the adults always whispered it whenever it was uttered.

Brian read about his childhood for another twenty minutes. His story startled me, not so much because of the poverty, but because he was so willing to reveal it. Like the rest of us, Brian earned enough money to live in a modern high-rise with twenty-four-hour security guards and a cleaning staff so attentive they even dusted our apartment doors.

When he finished reading, Brian looked up from his laptop and gently closed the cover. We sat in silence. And then the questions began.

"What was that like, being so hungry as children?"

"How did your mom manage?"

"Do you have any relationship with your dad these days?"

We had plenty of questions, but none of us asked Brian why he was writing in the third person. That question wouldn't come until we'd been writing and reading for each other for several years. One night, we heard Brian use personal pronouns for the first time. All of us noticed the transition—all of us, except Brian, who laughed in genuine surprise when someone mentioned it.

"I guess I was hiding in plain sight, trying to erase my past—from myself and everyone else," Brian reflected. "The only way for me to begin to show you my life was to write about it in the third person. But I guess that's changed now."

From the earliest meeting, Writers' Group was a place where we began to lay down a pattern for our friendship, interweaving threads of trust as we listened to one another's stories and asked questions, doing our best to provide answers.

That first reading session, we stood with Rachel on the porch of her childhood house in the parched city of Los Angeles, licking our lips as we sensed her craving for the desert's infrequent rains. We felt the prick of scorched grass under our feet, then breathed a collective sigh of relief as the skies finally opened and we watched a pint-sized Rachel dancing and leaping with delight through the raindrops. She'd written less than a page, but the images remain with me today.

My new friends walked with me along my happy childhood street in small-town Newfoundland. Listening, my friends discovered I was well into my adult years before I realized that nearly every house, including my own, sheltered an unmentionable crisis:

a son's drug addiction, a husband's alcoholism, a mother's suicide, an infant's death. I concluded my story with this line:

> When I was a kid, I thought my neighborhood was idyllic. It wasn't until I grew up that I realized it was normal.

It was 10 p.m. when we finally turned off the lights in the dining room and headed upstairs to our apartments. I unpacked the wicker basket I used to carry things from my apartment, returning cheese to the fridge and crackers to the cupboard. Before I went to bed, I sent a quick text message to Rachel.

"I am still trying to grasp what happened tonight. It felt like we were on sacred ground."

She texted me back: "I love our friends."

Childhood neighborhoods shape you for life. I grew up in a family—and on a street of families—defined by good manners and polite conversation. Filters were as highly valued as a tidy front lawn. There was a reason I was well into my adult years before I understood the troubled realities of so many of the families on my street. No one ever shared family secrets.

Not so for Rachel and Brian. Sure, they had good manners, and they knew how to engage in polite conversation. But neither of them had much time for superficiality. Had I insisted on remaining in the shallows, they'd have disappeared from my life pretty quickly. But they were patient with me and generous, telling their own stories, risking revelation, and wooing me out to deeper waters.

It wasn't easy for me to follow them. What about the private, intimate pieces of my life? What about my hopes and desires, my embarrassments and irrational fears? What about my lack of experience in what I considered the wilder side of life? I'd never used drugs, had always cut my alcohol off before I was under its influence, and had rarely attended parties where all limits were off. I haven't had much experience with love affairs. I can count the men

I've dated on one hand and have only once truly fallen in love. I'd never been fired from a job, and I've only lost one friend through unresolved conflict. Would the unfiltered me be interesting enough to sustain friendships with people like Rachel and Brian, people who had experienced so much that I had not?

I wasn't sure. But I was determined to open myself up to the possibility. Writers' Group would be one of my proving grounds. My friendship with Brian, another.

Pain and Pleasure

*T*here is a rare category among humans when it comes to friendship. These are the kind of people who pursue new friends with a dogged hopefulness. Like puppies with a tennis ball, they'll catch every toss and bring it back, over and over again. If you stop throwing the ball, they'll nudge your foot repeatedly until you notice.

Rachel was like that. So was Brian. Three days after they met in the hot tub, he was cooking breakfast for her. The day after I met him at Writers' Group, he sent me an email, attaching an article he thought I'd find interesting. Over the course of the next two weeks, while he was traveling, he sent seven more. In the first five years of our friendship, he sent at least seven hundred emails, many of them written while he was on vacation or away for work. In nearly all of them he wanted to share an idea or an opinion, a link to an article, or a photo of some expensive meal he was eating at that precise moment. Brian was always offering up food for thought.

A week after Writers' Group, Rachel cooked dinner for Brian and me at her apartment. We perched on her red vinyl bar stools, leaning elbows on the counter while she stood on the other side, chopping chives and parsley. Nearby, the crockpot simmered, infusing the room with scents of curry, turmeric, and ginger. Outside, the night was dark and cold, but we were tucked inside, feeling at home in Rachel's space.

It felt safe. Perhaps that is why our conversation so quickly turned to our beliefs about God.

"I believe in God," said Brian, "but I haven't always. Actually, it was here, in this neighborhood where I encountered God." He went on to recount how he'd been rollerblading one August afternoon when his feet flew out from under him and he landed flat on his back.

"I was laid up for a month after that, didn't see a doctor, peed into a bucket by my bed, eventually was able to crawl around my apartment on my hands and knees. There was nobody to help me. As I began to feel better, I'd go out on my balcony every morning and every night, just looking out over the lake. That's where I discovered nature. I was mesmerized. It occurred to me that only God could do that."

"I believe in God too," I said. "Nature is part of that, but Jesus also figures in it for me."

Brian shook his head. "I don't believe in Jesus."

"Not even as a historical figure?" I asked. "There's a lot of evidence for that."

"Nope, not at all."

"Have you ever read anything about him? Read any of his teachings?"

"Why would I? He never existed."

Brian and I batted the idea of Jesus between us like a ping-pong ball as Rachel, silently observing our match, continued to chop and stir. Eventually she placed bowls of sweet, thick vegetable curry in front of us.

"You could explore the idea of him, read about him as if you are reading a fantasy novel or science fiction," I suggested. Brian just shook his head and swallowed a heaping spoonful of curry.

"This is amazing," he said to Rachel.

A week later, Brian cooked for Rachel and me, inviting us into his twenty-third-floor apartment and taking us further into the story of his life. A narrow hallway carpeted with Persian rugs stretched from the main door toward his living room. On the walls, he'd hung military certificates, commendations for twenty-five years of service. As we walked down the hall, Brian opened doors along the way.

"I want to show you inside this room," Brian said, leading us into a small space. Shelves ran along two walls, and a wooden desk was pushed against the floor-to-ceiling window. Every surface was filled with photographs and memorabilia from Brian's life—passports, rings, letters, trophies. As we walked slowly around the room, he picked up various objects, telling us the story behind them: the ring belonging to his brother, who had died from AIDS; a newspaper clipping about his grandmother, who set numerous Canadian swimming records and was nearing her one hundredth birthday; his own high school sports trophies; a photo of his mother.

"This stuff was all in boxes," he told us. "I've hauled them around with me for thirty years but when I moved here, I finally decided to unpack them, to look at my life. I hadn't talked to my mom in fifteen years, hadn't said 'I love you' in fifty. I've done that now, said 'I love you' to my mom and meant it."

During my journalism career, many people had shared parts of their lives with me, trusting me to tell their stories faithfully to others. But I'd never met anyone like Brian, so eager to expose so much of his life so quickly with no formal reason attached to his revelations. His transparency intrigued me, which was a good thing because that night, and in the nights to come, he tossed plenty of explosive revelations my way, any one of which might have sent me scurrying away from relationship with him, not further into it.

Later that evening, as we sat in Brian's living room—stomachs full from second helpings of beef roulade, roasted potatoes, and asparagus—our conversation turned again to ideas about God and then, to what we believed about evil. Once again, we were sparring: Brian argued for an evolutionary and biological basis for evil, while Rachel and I attributed it to a spiritual force.

"Here, take this and read it," Brian said, handing me a dog-eared book called *The Dark Side of Man.* "It will help you understand my point of view."

Had I read the book (which suggests that male violence—even rape—is biologically rooted and tied to an innate need to procreate), I might have been better prepared for our next conversation. Instead, I placed *The Dark Side of Man* on top of a stack of other books on my living room windowsill, thinking I'd get to it eventually. I never did; I never really needed to. Brian was about to provide me with more than enough education on that subject and many others too.

On a Sunday evening in mid-December, Brian arrived at my door with a vintage bottle of pinot noir: expensive, full-bodied, and delicious. We finished it over the course of two or three hours, maybe more, without either of us noticing.

Later that night, I wondered if, along with that bottle of wine, Brian had carried his own agenda into my living room: the education of Lynda.

Before that conversation, I'd heard (but never really believed) the statistic that a gay man could have five hundred or more sexual partners in the course of his lifetime. By the end of the night, I believed it to be true, at least in Brian's case. He proved it by telling me stories about his encounters in Greek bathhouses, Berlin sex clubs, and the shrubbery in Toronto's High Park.

The stories, shocking as they were, did not unhinge me as much as something Brian said later in the evening, after we'd moved on from his stories to explore the meaning beneath them. His tales were often jarring, their edges sharp with descriptions of rough sex and drug overdoses. He'd ended up in hospital emergency rooms a couple of times, not sure of where he'd been, who he'd been with, or what had happened to his body.

"It doesn't sound very pleasant," I said at one point. "It sounds really painful."

"Pain and pleasure," he responded. "Aren't they the same thing?"

I stared at Brian, speechless for a few moments. "Are you kidding me? No, I don't think they are the same thing at all. Do you seriously believe that?"

After Brian left, I sat for a long time on the couch, staring across the room at my reflection in the window, the night as incomprehensible as our conversation. *Was he right? Were pain and pleasure the same thing? Had I just not opened myself up to enough experiences in life to know that?*

No. There was something skewed about his view. It seemed to me he was buying into a lie.

We were so different, Brian and me. Our beliefs, choices, and life experiences so vastly at odds.

I had many questions, but surprisingly, whether or not to continue in friendship with Brian wasn't one of them. I didn't much like some of his stories. But I quite liked him.

And so I wasn't really surprised when, a few weeks later, Brian and I ended up spending an entire Saturday together. I had in mind an hour-long jaunt along the lakeside trails in front of our building. Although it's reclaimed land—mostly created by mounds of excess concrete, stone, and imported topsoil—the area is wild and feels natural, full of blackbirds, cardinals, and meadowlarks. In the spring, red-necked grebes nest in holding ponds that filter the waters of Lake Ontario, and trumpeter swans patrol the shoreline. Graveled trails wind their way through sumac, wild rhubarb, and willow, leading out to a small beach where flotsam drifts in to stoke campfires all summer long. The landscape shifts with the seasons, and you never know quite what you'll find as you round a corner. I loved discovering its surprises.

We set out midmorning and walked through the trails for a while, then headed west along the lake, past more high-rises, some smaller apartment buildings, and a few lanes of row houses. We stopped to take selfies in front of a marina where boats slept through the winter.

"Let's keep going," Brian said. "I have to pick up my dry-cleaning, and it's not far from here." So we kept walking, heading away from the lake toward a stretch of shops: a small grocery store, Indian and Thai takeaway restaurants, a café, and, finally, the laundry where Brian stopped to pick up his washed and pressed dress shirts. While we were there, he introduced me to the woman behind the counter. He knew her by name.

He also called the proprietor of the Indian restaurant by name when we stopped there so he could pick up some food for dinner later that night. "Join me," Brian suggested, "I'll get enough for two." And he proceeded to order butter chicken, garlic naan, rice, and *paneer kheer*, his favorite sweet and milky dessert.

My hour-long jaunt was stretching well beyond what I'd had in mind, but I said yes to dinner, thinking I'd have the afternoon to myself before reconnecting with Brian for the evening. I liked the way my day was shaping up.

As we headed east toward our building, I mentioned I had a few errands to run that afternoon and would need my car. "I'll come with you," Brian quickly offered.

And so off we went, stopping at a butcher shop, where Brian hugged me as he joked with the man behind the counter. "This is my wife. We're out and about for the day. She doesn't like it when I hug her in public."

I rolled my eyes and asked for a half pound of bacon as Brian kept up his banter, making me laugh out loud more than once.

That Saturday, Brian and I spent ten hours together, beginning with our walk through the nature trails in the morning and ending with our feast of Indian food in the evening. The whole day, not just the meal, had been spicy and rich. I can recall many of the conversations Brian and I have had through the years of our friendship, but when I think about that day, our laughter is what first comes to mind.

Laughter. And then the sobering lesson God had for me.

I was still in the early days of trying to figure out what it meant to love my neighbors, but on that day, with Brian, I realized I was operating under some faulty presuppositions. I wanted to do things on my terms and at my speed. I thought an hour-long walk with Brian was generous. After that I would be entitled to the rest of my day and the tasks I wanted to accomplish. I can't for the life of me remember what they were now, but at the time they seemed quite important.

"The command to love," writes author Leon Morris, "gives food for thought because in the way we commonly use the term love, the response cannot be commanded. It is drawn from us. . . . We fall in love, we do not think of ourselves as in charge of the process."[1]

I'd begun that Saturday carefully dispensing the time I would give to Brian, wanting to be in charge of my day. Brian was having none of that—he wanted to spend the whole day with me. I suspect God was siding with Brian as a way of giving me time and space to discover why loving my neighbor was a good thing. Except, on that day, I wasn't thinking about theological questions at all. When I couldn't come up with a good reason to say no to Brian's invitations, I simply said yes instead.

Making Gnocchi

*B*rian always seemed to be bringing me gifts: a mosaic wall tile purchased in a Turkish bazaar; a garish orange handbag from New York's LaGuardia Airport; and, my favorite, a black-paged journal that came with a white gel pen. As I wrote in the journal, watching my words form jet trails across the pitch-black pages, I often felt like I was in a conversation with Brian, moving from dark places into light as we wrestled with ideas and perspectives.

But, as with Rachel, the best gifts Brian brought into my life were people, the strangers he met and invited into our lives. Some of them, including his lovers from Spain, Mexico, and Egypt, came and went. We'd welcome them to Monday night dinners, sometimes even to Writers' Group. They'd be around for a season, and then they'd be gone. But other people, neighbors like Anna and Ron, remained.

Brian met Anna on the elevator one evening about a month after we'd started Writers' Group. They were both bundled up against the cold: he was heading across the city to play badminton; she was going only as far as the back of the building to take her beagle for a walk. By the time they'd descended twenty floors, Brian had discovered quite a bit about Anna: her dog's name was

Lilly and, yes, Lilly always wore pearls; Anna and her husband, Ron, had recently moved to Toronto from Connecticut for his one-year work contract; Anna wasn't working and was slightly bored; she was also on the mend from recent knee surgery.

"Call my friend Rachel," said Brian, not one to observe the animal-only introduction rule when riding elevators. He scribbled a phone number on a scrap of paper and handed it to Anna. "She's into fitness and can help you out. Plus, we've started a writing group. You should come to that."

Anna never did call Rachel about her knee, but a month later, she mustered the courage to come to Writers' Group. Rachel and I were already in the room, the table spread with its usual feast. I still remember my elation when I saw Anna peeking around the door, brown eyes bright with expectation, her smile tentative but hopeful.

"As I came into the room, it really helped that I could tell you two were laughing and enjoying each other's company," Anna told me later when I asked what that first evening had been like for her. "You looked up and noticed me. I felt welcome the moment I walked through the door. And heck, there was a lot to eat and drink on that table! Who wouldn't feel welcome?"

As usual, Rachel and I had prepared for a crowd even though we knew Brian was away and we had no idea whether anyone else would come. We shared the philosophy that a bounty of good things to eat and drink provided a kind of edible welcome mat. That night, we'd set the table with crusty baguettes, a round of melted Brie, and a small dish of my homemade red pepper jelly. Rachel had wrapped a tea towel around a basket of samosas, keeping them warm until we were ready to slather them with spiced raisin chutney. We'd uncorked a bottle of red wine and had another bottle of white, plus Perrier, in reserve. Anna, it turned out, preferred white to red, and we were glad we could oblige her taste.

That night, it wasn't only Anna who needed comfort food. Our writing topic was *Our Greatest Fear,* and Rachel's story had brought tears to both our eyes. She cried as she read her piece; I cried as I listened. Refilling our plates provided a needed break before I read my story.

That's when Anna entered the room.

We made our introductions, and I explained what we were doing as Rachel uncorked the wine, pouring a glass for Anna.

"Why don't you reread your story," I suggested to Rachel.

Anna didn't say much after Rachel finished, never letting on whether or not she understood Rachel's story about her childhood and the oblique references to God as a gentle monster, one she desperately wanted to befriend, but whom she feared might forget her. Nor did Anna press me when I admitted in my story that I was afraid of many things—house fires, June bugs, roller coasters—and most of all, losing control.

Instead, Anna relaxed in her chair and took everything in. The next month, when we decided to revisit the topic of fear so we could hear from more people, Anna wrote about coming to Writers' Group. Then she went further and gave us glimpses of her life story. I wasn't totally surprised by her transparency—it was becoming the norm as we gathered each month around that dining room table. Her story was only 520 words long, and midway through, she read this:

> Why was I so afraid to come here tonight? All day I kept telling myself, "You can do this! You've overcome all kinds of obstacles." I've almost lost a child, giving me a whole new perspective on how valuable life is; I've been a care giver to my loving father for two years watching him slowly wither into someone who was no longer my witty, charismatic dad. I've moved ten times to five countries not knowing anyone and adjusted just fine. I'm currently dealing with having a son who

is suffering with schizophrenia. It's so heartbreaking to watch my bright, beautiful, kind child have an illness that can be treated but not cured and while treated changes the person he is meant to be . . . and I'm AFRAID to go to a Writers' Group?

In the months to come Anna would often begin with the disclaimer: "I'm not a writer. I'm just here for the company. And the wine."

We all disagreed. Month after month, she kept us entranced as she read stories of her life. Anna, it turned out, was a natural story-teller. Thanks to those stories we became increasingly eager to meet her husband, Ron, and were all a little jealous of Brian, who met him first.

They were introduced by way of a cabbage. One night as Writers' Group was ending, Anna asked if she could offload some groceries since she and Ron were going away for a few weeks. Brian said yes and even though it was after 11 p.m., Anna invited him up to her apartment to retrieve them.

Ron was already in bed when Anna and Brian came through the door.

"Come meet Brian," Anna called out.

"I'm not wearing any pants," Ron replied.

"That suits me just fine!" shouted Brian. He and Ron have been friends ever since. And the story of their meeting has become one of our legends.

But for a long time, the rest of us had to be satisfied with getting to know Ron on paper as Anna read story after story about their forty years of marriage. She started with their teenage romance and then bundled us into their station wagon so we could experience everywhere life took them after that. Anna's stories were nearly always about family life somewhere in the world—the New Jersey neighborhood of their first house, the cloistered compound in Pakistan where they introduced their two children to worldviews so very different than their own, favorite Disney vacations with their only granddaughter.

Anna mostly told happy, funny stories that made us laugh.

But every now and then she would step outside her carefully protected happiness zone and invite us to witness the chaos she knew existed, but preferred not to think about for too long.

"I considered Writers' Group my therapy session," she once said to me. "I opened up in there like I've never opened up, even with really good friends of mine. I'd just go into that dining room, and I'd let loose of all my inhibition and talk. It was almost like a confessional."

She had a point. Each month when we gathered in that first-floor dining room, the stories we read to each other transformed the nondescript room into a sacred space. The stories we shared, whether poignant, painful, or embarrassing, seemed full of truth. I, too, felt myself opening up a bit more, trying to reveal my truest thoughts, instead of guarding them in my own soul.

Month after month, as I witnessed people lay their stories on the table, I began to be dissatisfied with my own attachment to caution. But, still, I fought it, often edging close to exposing absolute truths about what I felt, thought, or believed, but not quite freefalling over the edge. I could tell when my friends were unsatisfied by my filtered offering, when they knew I was inching toward vulnerability but not quite landing there.

Gradually, I began to write with more courage. I stopped using my skillfulness with words as a way of making a point without revealing too much of myself. I began to gently set down my own stories, inviting friends and strangers to pick them up, turn them over in their hands—to tell me if they tasted truth.

I began to do this more and more—in the dining room where we met for Writers' Group, but also in my own living room. I began to open myself up because that's what I witnessed in my new friends—Rachel, Brian, Tanya, and Anna—and eventually Ron too.

"Let me teach you how to make gnocchi," Anna suggested to Rachel and me a couple of months after she'd started coming to Writers' Group. "I'll get all the ingredients and we can make it in my kitchen, then eat together. It will be delicious. Plus, I'll try to persuade Ron to join us so you can meet him."

When we arrived at their apartment, Anna and Lilly greeted us at the door, our friend in a festive apron, the dog in her pearls. As the dog ran circles around our feet, Anna encircled us with hugs.

"Here, I got you both aprons," she said as we made our way toward her galley kitchen. There was just enough space for the three of us to fit, me at the counter next to the window, Rachel working on the other side next to the stove, Anna hovering between us.

She'd bought us each a three-by-four-inch, ridged, wooden gnocchi board and patiently taught us how to place a tiny heap of potato and grated cheese on the center of a square of dough, then gently roll it down the board into a tidy (or in my case, not so tidy) little pouch. We were just beginning to drop the gnocchi into boiling water when we heard the apartment door open.

"Anna, I'm home." The voice coming from the hallway was tinged with traces of a New Jersey accent, evidence of their roots even though they'd lived all over the world. As Ron came into the apartment, we could hear him wheeling his bicycle into a small sitting area next to their front door. He biked most places in Toronto in sunshine and snow—across the city to the factory where he worked, along the bike paths in front our building, to his weekly Italian lessons. He biked in the early mornings before daylight, and late into the evening darkness.

Poking his head into the kitchen, he said a brief hello to us and shook his head at his dog. "Come on, Lilly," he coaxed the beagle, "they don't need you in the kitchen."

The four of us ate a slow and satisfying meal together that night, relishing the generous bowls of gnocchi drenched in olive oil and topped with fresh basil and grated Parmesan cheese. We were groaning about how full we were when Ron announced he'd brought dessert home with him.

"I'm so excited," he said. "I'm so glad Anna has met you guys and that you've become friends. I want to celebrate by sharing my most favorite dessert with you. And let me tell you, I've done my research. You won't get better than what I'm about to treat you with tonight." He rose from the table and headed back toward the door, retrieving a brown paper bag he'd left next to his bike.

"Butter tarts," he proclaimed as he opened the bag. "You haven't lived until you've tried these butter tarts. This has been such a great meal—gnocchi is the pasta version of my butter tarts—we have to finish this meal off in style. Besides, you deserve it," he continued, grinning at Rachel and me. "I'm so enamored by the fact that you both have loved learning to make something my family has been making since I was a little kid."

Years after Anna and Ron moved away from Toronto, he sometimes returned to the city for business trips. If he was in the city on a Monday night, he'd come back to our neighborhood, rarely appearing without a dozen butter tarts and never revealing how expensive they were. I once went in search of them and, discovering they were four dollars per tart, bought a much-cheaper cake instead. But Ron never balked at the price, he simply shared them around the room, brown eyes crinkling as he relished our enjoyment of something he loved.

Ron loved many things deeply: learning languages, pilgrimages to Iceland, riding his bike, reading books. He practiced a quiet faith, appreciating the silence of Quaker services. And Ron loved Anna. This was obvious in many ways, but the one that spoke significantly to me was the space he gave her around Writers' Group. He never attended, never asked her to read her stories, never worried that she was revealing so much about their lives to people they were just beginning to know.

"I didn't want to invade Anna's space," he told me when I asked him why he'd never joined us. And then, careful not to appear too magnanimous, he added, "there was a bit of selfishness involved too. I had places I didn't want her to invade either."

Over the years of our friendship, both Anna and Ron relaxed their boundaries. Ron never came to Writers' Group, but he regularly showed up at Monday night dinners. He was quick to offer their apartment as a place for summer barbecues, and it was his idea that Rachel, my marathon-running neighbor, Elizabeth, and even out-of-shape me, train and compete in a mini-triathlon. When he and Anna eventually moved to Connecticut, Rachel, Brian, and I made road trips to visit them. If Ron and Anna needed a place to stay on visits back to Toronto, they used my guest room.

Anna came to Writers' Group partly because Brian invited her, partly because Ron encouraged her, and partly because she wanted to make new friends in a new city. Friendship, with both Anna and Ron, settled easily into place.

But that wasn't the case with everyone. When I met Yolanda, it was immediately apparent she was no puppy eagerly nudging about for friendship.

Hugging Yolanda

If you are open to engaging anyone you bump up against in life—randomly or by choice—some people will easily become your friends. Others are prickly, and it will take time and patience to nudge your way in. I make friends easily, and I know in my own way, I'm a seeker of friendship. But generally, I've followed an evolutionary pattern, allowing relationships to take their course, waiting for the right moment to lean more deeply into a conversation, rather than pushing the quick-start button. This was not Brian's way. Brian was an instigator, an initiator, subscribing more to the Big Bang theory of friendship. He and Rachel were alike in this and often the ones who brought new people into the little community taking shape in our neighborhood.

It was because of Brian that Yolanda, and subsequently, her son Luka, found their way into our lives.

My first sighting of Yolanda was at the annual condo Christmas party. She was hard to miss, sparkling more than the twinkly lights strung on the artificial tree in our building's rooftop party room. She was wearing thigh-high gold lamé boots that accentuated her long, thin legs and a short, strapless dress. Curls of thick blonde hair fell almost to her waist, and when she smiled, it was wide, her teeth white and straight. Over the years, I would grow accustomed to seeing her fish dental floss from her purse and disappear into a bathroom or around a corner, anywhere she could find a mirror to examine her teeth. Yolanda was also always the first to alert someone else about wayward poppy seeds or flecks of spinach marring their smile.

I was chatting with Brian and Rachel when I noticed Yolanda across the room, wine glass in hand, holding court before a small circle of people. Had I stuck around as long as everyone else that night, we would have met each other. But I left the party well before my friends did. They had more stamina and, eventually, engaged in conversation with Yolanda.

A few months later when Brian organized dinner and a movie in our building's theater room, he invited Yolanda. There was nothing superficial about Brian's choice of movie—we watched *Trade*, a film about sex trafficking. Later, as we discussed the movie over the Indian takeaway food Brian provided, it became apparent Yolanda was not one for superficiality either. Even though she was new to our group, she was quick to engage anyone in debate and seemed sure of her opinions. We invited her to our next Writers' Group.

When Yolanda walked through the door of the dining room a week later, I threw open my arms and welcomed her with a hug. It was impulsive, not something I did with everyone, and I can't explain why I did it with her. But it was the right move. Yolanda hugged me back and immediately christened me her fairy godmother, a term I didn't exactly relish because it was too physically appropriate: my body is soft, squishy, and round. I'm short—only five-feet, three-inches—and there are plenty of laugh lines around my brown eyes. But Yolanda meant the term differently, telling me later that she sensed something warm and affectionate in my quick smile, a genuine welcome in the way I so readily opened my arms to her. Magical or miraculous, there was something in the air that evening because I am not generally given to hugging people, especially those I barely know.

But hugging quickly became the habitual greeting between the two of us, a relational expectation from Yolanda, even before she was willing to admit we were friends. And that took a long time.

More than a year after we first met, I was hosting Monday night dinner because Rachel was away. Yolanda, who by this time had become a Monday night regular, stayed later than everyone else. She usually pushed the limit, staying twenty or thirty minutes beyond our 9 p.m. curfew. Luka was with his father on Monday evenings, and Yolanda appreciated the opportunity to socialize with other adults.

I was rinsing dishes at the kitchen sink as she tidied the living room, plumping cushions on the couch, stacking coasters on a bookshelf, and bringing me wayward glasses people had left on windowsills.

"Thanks for helping clean up," I said to her as I added the glasses to the nearly full dishwasher. Then, grinning mischievously, I said: "Have I told you lately that I really appreciate your friendship?"

"Acquaintances," she replied. "That's what we are. Not friends. Acquaintances."

"You can call it whatever you want," I said. "But, by my definition, you're a friend." Then we hugged each other before she picked up her purse and headed out the door.

And I really did consider her a friend—whether she made me laugh, rethink my opinions, repeatedly explain myself, or keep my mouth shut—I enjoyed her company and appreciated what she contributed to our gatherings. This was not true for everyone. Sometimes Yolanda's unfiltered stories, insistent questions, and strong opinions would send neighbors home early from our Monday night dinners or even keep them away for a few weeks. Sometimes she annoyed me, too, but mostly, when her stories went on too long, I could tamp down my annoyance. I'd find a way to change the subject and bring order back to our little world. Mostly my strategy worked. Until it didn't.

After several months of meeting, our Writers' Group had expanded to seven, and the small, narrow room was feeling pleasantly full. Lots of beverages and plenty to eat helped people feel more relaxed, but one evening as the clock ticked past 9 p.m., I was feeling tense. Three people had yet to read their stories. It was going to be a long night, and I had to be up at 6:30 to prepare for work in the morning.

Nicolai, a recent member of the group who had joined us after meeting Rachel at the neighborhood bus stop, had just finished reading a poetic piece about a painting he'd seen in a museum. After we'd discussed his story for fifteen minutes, I suggested we should move on to the next writer.

"Wait," said Yolanda. "I have more questions."

"Perhaps you could ask them after we've finished hearing from everyone else," I suggested. "It's getting late and we still have more readers." Inwardly, I was also thinking she'd asked so many questions already I'd lost count.

"I want to ask them now," she replied. "Nicolai, I really want to understand more of what you are writing about."

"Sure," said Nicolai. "I don't mind."

"I really think we should move on," I interjected, keeping my voice level and polite. "To be fair to everyone. You are welcome to stay and ask Nicolai more questions after everyone has read."

"No. I am curious. I have questions I want to ask." Yolanda was insistent.

"But I think it would be better to allow someone else to read," I protested.

Ignoring me, Yolanda leaned across the table toward Nicolai. "Tell me more about what you were referring to when . . ."

I didn't hear the rest of her question. I was aware only of a tiny tornado of rage twisting inside me. I pressed my hands together on my lap and my lips together in a tight line across my face. I was sitting next to Yolanda, close enough to slap her. It took every ounce of my willpower not to do it.

"Yolanda," Tanya's voice was measured and calm. "I think you are making people uncomfortable. Let's move on."

"Oh, okay." And with that, Yolanda sat back and asked, "Who will read next?"

The evening was a late one; it was after 11 p.m. when we finally packed away leftover food and stacked the empty wine bottles on the floor of the adjoining kitchenette. When, finally, Rachel and I were alone in the elevator, I said, "That was a crazy night. Did you sense how angry I was at Yolanda?"

"I had an idea," Rachel replied. "Thank goodness for Tanya!"

And then we both started to laugh.

Early the next morning, I sat on my couch, watching as clouds scudded across the sky and snow fell on the frozen lake. *What*, I wondered, *had transpired the night before?* I doubted anyone in the dining room, except perceptive Rachel, had any inkling I was one slap away from ending any possibility of relationship with Yolanda. The fact that I'd preserved my reputation as a fairy godmother didn't console me; rather it made me feel like a hypocritical witch, craftily concealing my true nature.

I sipped my morning coffee and picked up my journal and began to write:

Why was I so angry last night? It only lasted a few moments, but it wasn't the span of time, it was the depth—even thinking about it now exhausts me. Do I want control of the group? See myself as somehow deserving of the position? I am the writer. I am experienced. I am older. I understand group dynamics. Is this my view of myself? Do I think I deserve this role?

And then, as is my habit, I wrote a short prayer in my journal:

> *God, show me how to grow in humility. Show me your love for my*
> *friends—Yolanda and others who press hard against me and cause*
> *eruptions in my spirit. Sometimes last night I felt like I was in a*
> *sacred space. At other times, I felt that space being trampled upon.*
> *But that is the lot of a human. We live in the sacred and we mar it.*

It would be five years before I told Yolanda about the night I wanted to slap her. As I had presumed, she'd had no idea I had been angry with her. Even though many years had passed and we'd truly become friends, she still felt the sting of that slap. "It's as if you really did it," she said.

"I know," I said. "I'm sorry. I'm really sorry."

In his Sermon on the Mount, Jesus teaches that thinking about something can be as real as doing it. He equates anger with murder, lust with adultery. I'd never fully understood how that could be, but now, thanks to Yolanda, I think I'm finally getting it. Wounding someone, whether in thought or action, is never a neutral act.

I do take some solace in the fact that I didn't actually slap Yolanda that night. Had I done so, I'm pretty sure she would have disappeared from my life. And that would be a great loss.

Two days after Writers' Group, oblivious to the anger I'd felt toward her, Yolanda invited me to dinner. It was not an invitation I would ever have expected. Earlier, during a Monday night dinner, she'd told us she hated cooking for people and found it hard to believe Rachel had no ulterior motives in cooking for a crowd week after week.

"I was expected to cook because I'm a woman," Yolanda told us. "I resent that. I heard it from my mom. I heard it from my husband. It's in my blood. So, for me to hear that someone loves cooking, it seems fake. Me, I hate hosting people. It's not that I hate the people who come. But my role is not to provide food. My role is only intellectual stimulation. That's the only thing."

In spite of what she said, on the night she hosted me, I discovered Yolanda was an excellent cook. She served me homemade borscht and a dill and cucumber salad, food from Ukraine, where she'd been born. By the time I met her, she'd been living in Canada for twenty years but had not lost her accent or her intuitive sense of just the right amount of pickle juice to add to a salad.

That evening I began to discover Yolanda's approach to parenting. The tidy apartment she shared with Luka was clearly the home of two intellectually curious and educated people, a mother and son who loved learning. Dinosaurs stalked across shelves and a planetary mobile swirled in the air over the kitchen counter. Little piles of fossils and shells, collected on the travels they regularly took around the world, were artfully arranged on shelves, tables, even on the bathroom vanity.

As soon as I arrived, Luka introduced me to his pet gecko, showing me how to let him perch on my shoulder and nestle into the hair at the back of my neck. I was surprised a dragon could have such a soft touch.

After dinner the three of us sat on their white leather couch and took turns shooting arrows across the room at a bull's-eye target drawn on the back of a pizza box. Luka was the best shot, Yolanda a close second. But I kept pace with them, even hitting the bull's eye once.

I stayed for a couple of hours. As I was leaving, Yolanda and I gave each other our customary hug, and then I turned to Luka and gave him one too.

Brunch with Jesus

For most of my life, I've relied on the Bible as my primary guide. Most days, I eat breakfast and drink my first coffee of the morning while reading and reflecting on a passage from the Old or New Testaments, overlaying it with a psalm to lead me into prayer. The Bible is a book that challenges, perplexes, rattles, and comforts me—sometimes all in the space of one reading. Six months after my dad's unexpected death in 2003, I found myself unable to find any solace in the Bible until a friend suggested I read only the psalms. I followed the advice, reading one psalm after another over the course of forty days, discovering in their ancient poetry a resting place for the anger and grief my dad's death had unearthed in me.

When I read and contemplate Scripture, my life begins to make more sense. This is true when I read it in solitude and when I read it in the company of others. I value communal conversations about the Bible because it helps me ponder my own questions as well as the ones I wouldn't necessarily unearth on my own.

I also love reading and studying the Bible with friends because I want everyone to discover what it has to say about the Creator of the universe. I want them to see how much God loves humans and this earth we inhabit. I want them to believe, as I do, that God helps us become fully alive here on earth, not only in heaven.

Years ago, I claimed an ancient idea as one of the rudders by which I steer my life: *the glory of God is a human fully alive.*

The saying, attributed to Saint Irenaeus, sums up one of my favorite biblical stories—the one about Jesus raising his friend Lazarus from the dead. When Jesus tells Martha, Lazarus's sister, that he will restore life to her dead brother, she responds, "I know he will rise again in the resurrection at the last day."

But Jesus answers: "I am the resurrection and the life. The one who believes in me will live, even though they die; and whoever lives by believing in me will never die" (John 11:23-44). At the tomb, Jesus calls: "Lazarus, come out!" And Lazarus, who's been wrapped head to toe in linens and buried for four days, is suddenly alive again. Later on, there's another story of Jesus eating a meal with Lazarus at the house he shared with Martha and their sister Mary. Oh, to be at that dinner party!

It starts now, I believe, this full life promised to Lazarus and Martha and Mary and anyone else who takes Jesus at his word. Reading the Bible is not the only way to fully understand life, but it provides wisdom I appreciate.

Three months into my friendship with Brian, I began to wonder if he would consider coming to a Bible study. We often had conversations about religion and faith, and even though he continued to be skeptical about Jesus, I had a feeling that if I invited him, he'd say yes. After all, he said yes to just about anything Rachel or I invited him to do. I hoped that if Brian began to read the Bible, he'd come to believe Jesus was real.

"What do you think about the idea of starting a Bible study?" I asked Rachel one morning as we sat in a coffee shop, about to begin our weekly prayer time. The initial floor party had gone well, people were beginning to show up for Monday night dinners, and we could both sense trust was growing through Writers' Group.

"Great idea. I'll come," she replied.

"But what about everyone else? Will they think I'm a fanatic if I invite them?" Our circle of acquaintances and friends had grown to more than a dozen people who had entrusted us with their email addresses.

"Just invite them, Lynda." It appeared Rachel didn't think we needed to pray about this decision. But I was still nervous. It was one thing to invite friends I'd known for years to a Bible study. Would I be breaking condo etiquette by inviting all my new neighbors to a religious activity?

The idea nagged at me until I finally gave into it a couple of weeks later on a wintery Saturday morning when I had nowhere else to be but in my own living room. Sitting at my dining table, laptop open before me, I thought for a while and then began to compose an email. After about ten minutes and lots of deleting, I typed, "Spiritual exercises for a new year," into the subject line.

"Just do it, Lynda." I heard Rachel's voice in my head and felt again her impatience with my timidity. "Who cares what people think?"

I began to type email addresses into the bcc line, starting with people who'd come to Writers' Group, then adding those who lived along the hallway beyond my apartment. Eventually, throwing all caution aside, I invited people I'd met at the gardening committee and at other building meetings. By the time I'd finished, there were fourteen names on the email.

I wrote a short note, mentioning Rachel's intention to be part of the study. Then I said a quick prayer and pressed send. In less than two minutes, I received my first reply. It was from Brian. My heart sank as I began to read.

Thoughtful of you to invite me, but no thanks . . . again, I am not sure about any religion at this time, never mind Jesus . . .

I sat for a few minutes pondering his response, when there was a knock at my door. *Who was coming by so early in the morning?*

I was still in my pajamas, so I slipped on my housecoat before peering through the peephole. Brian was standing in the hallway. Hair awry and wearing glasses instead of contact lenses, he didn't look much more put together than me, so I opened the door, not caring he'd caught me unprepared for company.

"I'm here for Bible study," he announced, striding into the room. "I was Skyping with my boyfriend when your email came, and I told him about your invitation, but that I wasn't going. He challenged me, said I was being a hypocrite. What did I know about the Bible? Why not learn something. So here I am!"

I began to laugh. I was laughing at my own fears, at Brian's impulsivity, and at the fact that his Muslim-born boyfriend was the one encouraging him to read the Bible. I was laughing at the sight of the two of us, me in my housecoat and slippers, still with bedhead and wearing no makeup, he in shorts and a T-shirt, so eager not to be a hypocrite that he'd missed half the details of my invitation.

"Well, I'm delighted," I said. "But Bible study doesn't start until *next* Saturday."

"What? Jesus Christ! Are you serious?" Brian started laughing, but not at the irony of his expletive. I smiled, let the words pass, and said, "No worries. I'm free later today if you want to get together. I should probably get dressed at some point."

No one else was as quick to respond to my invitation. A few people politely declined, but most simply ignored it. Everyone still said hello to me in the elevators; nobody shunned me because of my religious effrontery. Initially, it looked like it would just be Brian, Rachel, and me. But, to my delight, the Bible study group began to take shape, not so much because I sent an email, but because Brian began inviting people.

"Hey, we have a Bible study," he'd say whenever someone new showed up at Monday night dinner. "I'm not religious—I'm just interested in history. You should come."

Yolanda accepted his invitation, and then began inviting new people too.

"Hey, we have a Bible study," she'd say. "I'm not religious—I'm just interested in the social connection and intellectual discussion. You should come."

In the end, there were usually six of us: me, Brian, Yolanda, Anna, Rachel, and Nicolai. Anna said yes because she'd attended Bible studies in the past and, although she wasn't attending church in those days, she missed conversations about faith. Nicolai was on his own spiritual journey; he'd lived in Croatia until he was thirteen and his family immigrated to Toronto. During his university studies in philosophy, he'd become interested in the writings of Kierkegaard and Kant, which set him on a spiritual quest as he compared their writings to his experiences in a society shaped by communism and atheism. When Rachel invited him to the Bible study, he said yes immediately.

Every now and then someone else would join our study for a while—Miraz, a Kazak-born security guard in our building invited by Nicolai; Pete, a neighbor who lived on the sixth floor of our building and had come into my life through the introduction of a mutual friend; Silvio, a Guatemalan immigrant who had propositioned Brian on a bus. In those days, Brian was choosing monogamy and so opted to invite Silvio to Bible study rather than into his bedroom.

But mostly it was just the six of us—Rachel, Nicolai, Brian, Anna, Yolanda, and me—sitting around my living room for three to four hours every Saturday, reading and discussing the Gospel of John while we drank coffee and ate from the smorgasbord of food everyone brought with them as they came through my door.

There were two other important regulars, although they never participated in the study. One was Luka, Yolanda's son, who would set himself up at my dining room table, quietly writing out

Ukrainian grammar lessons in a notebook until he'd earned his mother's approval and could watch nature documentaries on his tablet. Every now and then, he'd lift his head and ask his mother a question in Ukrainian. We'd pause our discussions, wait for their brief, mysterious conversation to conclude, and then pick up where we'd left off.

The other was Jewel, Brian's twelve-year-old parrot. She'd enter the room perched on his shoulder and mostly stay there. But sometimes she'd take flight, land on someone else, or strut around the apartment as if she owned the place. I always draped towels over my furniture when Jewel came to visit. She never contributed to the discussion, but she left her mark in other ways.

Our approach to the study was simple: we printed out the Gospel of John on sheets of paper rather than using bound Bibles. This way people could make notes and mark it up. To begin, we'd read a page or two out loud and then everyone would spend ten minutes or so reading silently, writing down the ideas or questions that surfaced as they contemplated the text. Then, one by one we would each voice two or three questions, which I would write down so we could work our way through them. Our conversation took flight like a kite on the wind. I never knew where it would take us.

Over the course of our studies, I was intrigued by the way people handled their sheaf of paper almost as much as I was by the questions they asked and the observations they made. For many weeks, Yolanda refused to write anything on the margins of her paper, holding all her questions in her head. "I don't want to make any mistakes," she would protest when I encouraged her to mark up the pages.

Rachel brought her own set of fine-point Sharpies, offering everyone their choice of colors. "Hello, Mr. Orange," she'd say to the marker, "Let's be friends today!" The more trust grew among us, the more Rachel let her inner child emerge. Ron once declared she could be as enthusiastic about doorknobs and flies as she could be about people. Her stories and antics made us laugh and released our own silliness.

Brian grabbed whatever pen or pencil was closest to him and scribbled his observations and questions along the margins, between the lines, on the backs of the pages, wherever he could cram them in. Most people took their pages home with them at the end of the study, but not Brian. Initially, he'd hand them back to me; apologetically admitting he was sure to lose them if he took them home. Eventually, he'd just leave them under his chair without apology, trusting I'd keep them until the next week. His sheaf of papers are still tucked away somewhere in my apartment.

Like Writers' Group, it didn't take many weeks for us to settle into preferred seats. Rachel and Nicolai on one end of the couch, Anna nestled into the other, and Yolanda in the middle, with enough room on either side of her for Luka to snuggle against her at any given moment. Brian always sat in an armchair, and I'd pull out one of the upholstered chairs from my dining room table.

Some mornings, Nicolai arrived with freshly made *burek*, a Croatian pastry dripping with cheese and butter his mom had taught him to make. Brian invariably brought us protein: spare ribs or octopus grilled on the barbecue he wasn't supposed to have on his balcony. Anna would bake muffins or pick up chocolate-dipped strawberries from our neighborhood patisserie.

In the early months of our meetings, Yolanda usually arrived with a big bottle of tomato juice or a couple of small frozen pizzas, which she'd pop into my oven regardless of how much food was already on the table. She was always sharing food with us that she'd found for bargain prices. As she became more comfortable, she began showing up with her own homemade salads. If Rachel contributed a bowl of hardboiled eggs, Yolanda would intercept her so she could peel, slice them in half, and slather them with mayonnaise. "This," she would say, "is how eggs are meant to be eaten."

Rachel always supplied a carafe of coffee, which Brian and Nicolai appreciated, but the rest of us politely declined. Yolanda kept a jar of instant coffee and a bottle of honey in my cupboard rather than carry them to and from her apartment every Saturday. I set my own coffee pot brewing, put the kettle on, and set out a box of Earl Grey tea for Anna.

Coffee and tea were our beverages of choice, but every now and then we found reason to include a more celebratory drink. The day we studied the passage about Jesus turning water into wine, we drank mimosas. We popped the cork on another bottle of champagne when we reached the end of John's Gospel, twenty-two months after we'd first begun.

Mimosas aside, our condo Bible study was the least orthodox one I'd ever attended. By the time we were into our second summer, I felt well enough connected to my neighborhood to increase my involvement at church. When Pastor Jim asked if I'd lead a Bible study for university students, I said yes and began to meet weekly at the picnic table on the church lawn, eating pizza and letting stories of Jesus lead us into conversation about faith and life.

"What's the difference between our study and the one at your condo?" one of the students asked me one evening.

"Well, for one thing," I replied, "there's a lot more swearing."

At the condo Bible study, the name Jesus Christ was frequently invoked, sometimes mindlessly, sometimes as an exclamation of anger, and sometimes in admiration. On one memorable morning, frustrated by the inconsistencies Brian saw between the story we were reading and the way life generally worked itself out, he slouched back in his chair, lifted his left arm, and angrily gave God the finger. On another morning he declared Jesus an admirable leader.

Swearing wasn't the only evidence of honesty. One morning, we spent a long time talking through the Gospel story of the dinner party at the home of Lazarus, Mary, and Martha. During the dinner, Mary pours expensive perfume on Jesus' feet and leans in

close, wiping them with her hair. It's not a small dinner party—
Jesus' disciples are also in the room and, one of them, Judas, criti-
cizes Mary for her wastefulness.

What would it be like, my neighbors and I wondered, to witness
such an intimate act at one of our dinner parties? Who, I asked my
friends, would you be most like?

Yolanda's response was quick. "I'd be Mary," she declared. "If
I was committed to Jesus like she was, I'd do exactly what she
did. It wouldn't matter what people thought. I'd be all in." None
of us disagreed.

Each Saturday morning before my friends arrived, I'd prepare
my house for their arrival, running the vacuum, dusting tables. I'd
bake a quiche or buttermilk biscuits and set out plates and cups,
Yolanda's coffee, and Anna's Earl Grey tea. Then, thirty minutes
before they arrived, I'd sit on my couch and pray for my friends. I
wanted so much for them to know God's love and to discover that
following Jesus was the best way to make it through this life. I
wanted them to be committed to Jesus, just like Mary was. Just like
Rachel and I were.

There's a photo taken on the last day of our Bible study when
we'd come to the end of John's Gospel. We're holding up champagne flutes, and we're all smiling. I suppose most of my friends
were glad to have accomplished what we'd set out to do—read
through and discuss an entire book of the Bible. I was also happy
we'd done that, but my smile masked a sadness.

"What difference does it make to you that you've read this book?"
I'd asked my friends that day. "Who is Jesus to you now?" An uncomfortable silence descended on the room, broken when Brian
stood up and said, "I don't want to answer that."

I was grieved that all my friends did not seem to be finding in
Scripture the anchor it had become for me. How could I find so
much spiritual meaning in the stories of Jesus, while Brian would

concede only that there were good leadership lessons to be learned? How was it I claimed God as the center of my life, when week after week Yolanda declared (not entirely in jest): "I am the center of my own universe."

I pondered my friends' declarations, and ultimately let my grief resolve into prayer. I prayed that my friends and I would continue to have conversations about faith, even though we'd finished the Bible study. I prayed they would never forget the stories and teachings of Jesus, but that they would surface, bidden or unbidden, when most needed. I prayed that they would press into the things they said they were beginning to believe—in Yolanda's case, that she could pray in the name of Jesus. In Brian's, that Jesus actually walked this earth, that he said some things well worth considering.

I prayed for patience for myself and for trust that God was at work in my friends' lives, whether I could see it or not. I prayed they would become fully alive.

Feasting with Babette

*Y*olanda called them our own holy trinity, those Monday night dinners, Saturday morning Bible studies, and monthly Writers' Group. And, like the actual Trinity, each had a role to play in seeding, strengthening, and sustaining the relationships between us. From the very beginning, there was a common theme in everything we did, a sacrament we practiced regardless of the purpose, the time, or the place of any particular gathering.

Always, we feasted. Food was essential.

A couple of years into our friendship, I booked our building's theater room and invited my friends to watch my favorite movie, *Babette's Feast.* I love the movie for many reasons, not the least of which is the leading role food plays in bringing a broken community together, healing decades-old wounds between neighbors, stirring up laughter and mischief where before there had been only grudges and disapproval. Our little group of friends had not experienced the same degree of communal brokenness, although our individual rough edges inevitably caused hurt and pain among us.

When I invited my friends to watch the movie with me, I wasn't trying to draw similarities between the Academy Award-winning Danish film and our own neighborhood life. I simply wanted to share a movie I loved with my friends, never dreaming Brian would lift my appreciation for the movie's truth to a whole new level.

"We should replicate this," Brian declared after we switched on the lights in the theater. Half a dozen friends had come to watch the movie and, once it ended, we leaned across the padded wooden seats and shifted our attention from the screen to one another. We spent an hour or so talking about the meaning of the grand feast the mysterious and exotic French woman named Babette prepared for the austere and frugal Danish community where she unexpectedly found herself living.

"I'll host the next Monday night dinner," Brian offered. "I'll serve you all a feast like Babette's."

I was not surprised by his offer. He loved to cook, telling me once that he approached cooking like he approached sex.

"When I pick up men, I want every one of them to say 'you're the best I've ever had.' It's the same with food. If I'm going to cook, I'm going to do it right, and I'm going to try not to take any shortcuts. I'm going to bring the whole of me into the room. Of course, the downside is it takes time, all the shopping for the stuff, preparing the food, cleaning up afterwards."

A week after the movie, we gathered in Brian's apartment for dinner. As we settled in, some people sitting on his leather club chairs, others on the couch against the window, a few more on the floor, Brian kept busy behind the kitchen counter, lifting the lid on a big soup pot, spooning it into bowls. The smell of salty fish began to permeate the room.

"Don't start until I've served everyone," he said. "We all have to try this at the same time."

No one was about to argue with him. In fact, as we each received our bowl, we weren't sure we actually wanted to spoon the lumpy, greyish-brown sludge into our mouths. Well, everyone except Rachel and Yolanda, who were always game to try anything.

"You made the soup!" Rachel exclaimed. "This is so great!"

In the movie, Babette's great feast of exotic cheeses, turtle soup, and roasted guinea hens is a climax. Another, more basic soup plays a supporting role. Made from salt fish, stale bread, and ale, the soup is the pitiful mainstay of the poor villagers until Babette arrives and begins to improve its taste by flavoring it with herbs and her own culinary skills.

We eyed our bowls with skepticism and then, in unison, dipped our spoons into what seemed more like porridge than soup. Immediately, there was grimacing and sputtering, wry faces, scrunched up noses.

"Did you soak the fish?" I asked Brian, already guessing by the intense saltiness what Brian's answer would be.

"Was I supposed to?" he asked innocently. Then he laughed. "Here, give me back your bowls. Don't eat it—even though I spent hours scouring Kensington Market for that fish!" Then he turned, opened his fridge, and lifted out a platter of Danish cheeses.

"I couldn't replicate Babette's whole feast, so I made stuffed pork loin with roasted vegetables. You have to try the crackling on the pork. I worked hard on that. And there's apple strudel for dessert. But we'll start with cheese."

With relief, we all handed our bowls back to Brian—except Yolanda, who finished the whole salty bowl of sludge, and then said to Brian: "Don't throw the rest out. I'll take it home with me." But the soup got the better of even frugal Yolanda. Months later, she confessed she could not stomach it and eventually threw it out.

"Food is symbolic," Rachel once said to me when I asked her why she was so committed to cooking for everyone on Monday nights. "Not necessarily for everyone, but for me. It's a picture of abundance, diversity, something truly pleasurable. It's also a way of serving each other, inviting each other into something."

Eventually, rather than bringing something she'd purchased—frozen pizza, a box of ice-cream bars, a jug of tomato juice—Yolanda began to prepare food for us. First, it was a homemade salad: cucumber, egg, and tomato chopped into tiny, symmetrical pieces. Then a pot of borscht or a thick soup seasoned with chicken livers and onions. Everything she made had obviously taken her some time to prepare.

"Yolanda often seemed afraid, like she would be judged by not being a good enough cook, for not getting things quite right," reflected Rachel. "She was surprised we loved her cooking so much."

Rachel, the generous host of our Monday night dinners, never tried to replicate Yolanda's salads or Brian's grilled ribs. She didn't need to; she had her own repertoire of recipes. Often, she'd study cookbooks for hours looking for something new to create. Then she'd spend most of her Sunday shopping and preparing the meal for the next evening.

Rachel rarely deviated from instructions. Much to her consternation, that was not my style. Once, when she didn't feel up to cooking, I took all the ingredients she had already purchased and prepared the meal. As she was leaving my apartment that Monday night, I handed her a bunch of parsley, half an onion, and two lemons.

"Why are these ingredients left over?" she asked, clearly perplexed.

"Well, you know me, I never follow a recipe exactly," I replied. She simply shook her head and never asked me to take over cooking one of her recipes again.

Rachel had to be ill before she'd relinquish Monday night meals to anyone else. She saw cooking for friends and inviting them to dinner as an act of service. And she loved hosting.

"When you bring yourself to my house, it's a way of saying you are bringing something of value," she said. "I want to give something back. I'm getting something from your presence, and I want to serve you with this gift of food. I want people to be well fed, not to be hungry. I want eating together to be a joyful experience."

Rachel wasn't the only one who felt that way. Anna also loved turning food into a gift, and spent hours one Monday concocting five different Indian recipes. When she was finished cooking, she wrapped the bowls and pots in towels to keep them hot as she carried them down ten floors to Rachel's apartment where the rest of us waited. And while her husband, Ron, left most of the cooking in their family to Anna, he clearly shared the philosophy of food as gift, proving it to a small group of us on a particularly memorable weekend.

Ron had been competing in triathlons for a number of years and was particularly impressed by Elizabeth's success at becoming a marathon runner. He knew I was also trying to get my body in better shape. One Monday, he suggested we enroll in a summer triathlon that offered varying levels of competition. Rachel and Elizabeth immediately said yes. I was less enthusiastic but eventually registered too.

A year after the triathlon, I asked Ron his favorite memories of that August weekend, and he said he had a few: he and Rachel unaware they'd won medals until they heard their names proclaimed through the loudspeaker; me finally crossing the finish line, last, but triumphant; our post-race breakfast; the gifts of running belts and energy bars he surprised us with the night before the race. But his favorite memory? The carbohydrate-rich dinner he cooked for us the night before the race. And the olives that took center stage.

"I remember asking you what Elizabeth would like, because I'd never seen her eat," Ron said to me. "And you said, 'Olives. She'll eat olives.'"

"So, I went to the market and I bought everything I needed to prepare supper for the rest of us—fresh pasta, pesto, chicken. And fire-roasted olives—those were for Elizabeth," Ron said, adding, "The top-off to that evening was that Elizabeth ate the whole supper and took home the leftovers. The olives worked.

"I get a kick out of Elizabeth," Ron said. "I love the way small things make her happy, like butter tarts, cherry cola, and olives. Not that she indulges very often in butter tarts or cherry cola. But if she wanted them, I'd be her supplier." And that, in fact, was what he'd become. Often, when Ron and Anna traveled to the United States, they'd return carrying a box of cherry cola to leave at Elizabeth's door.

Rachel and I also supported and respected Elizabeth's discipline about food. Sometimes she'd ask me to store a butter tart in my freezer for months on her behalf. Better my freezer than hers, she'd say. As disciplined as she was, butter tarts within too close a proximity could get the better of her. Chocolate too. Whenever someone gave Elizabeth chocolate, she'd carry it down the hallway to Rachel's apartment, where it had its own space on a kitchen cupboard shelf.

Ron never expected Elizabeth to eat the full meal with the rest of us the night before the triathlon. The olives were his way of inviting her to be fully present at the table, but on her terms.

"I admire what she has done, all the weight she has lost and how she's taken on running," Ron told me. "She's gone from being at a level of health she wasn't happy with to being an instructor for runners. I really like that about her."

"Why did you eat Ron's dinner that night?" I asked Elizabeth one Friday evening as she, Rachel, and I sat chatting in my living room. She was drinking carbonated water, Rachel had made herself a martini, and I'd poured myself a glass of merlot. On the coffee table in front of us there was a round of Brie, a hunk of smoked cheddar, and slices of salami. There was also a bowl of mixed olives I'd purchased at a deli on my way home earlier that evening.

"Which ones should I buy?" I'd asked the deli manager as I surveyed the trays of olives in front of me—brown kalamatas, bright green castelvetranos, fat cerignolas stuffed with cream cheese, wrinkled black nyons infused with oregano and thyme, petit picholines, and, my favorites, purple gaetas.

"Take the mix," he advised. "That way you get to try them all."

I watched as Elizabeth leaned forward in her chair, surveyed her options, choosing first a castelvetrano, then a picholine. She popped them, one after another, into her mouth and chewed slowly, savoring the saltiness.

Then she sat back and reflected on my question.

"Why did I eat Ron's meal that night? Because he was so excited to offer it to us, because he'd gone to such trouble to make the weekend so special. Because I knew it would make him happy. I really admire him."

"Did you really eat the leftovers you took home?" Rachel asked.

"I probably threw them out," she confessed. "But don't tell Ron. I wouldn't want to hurt his feelings."

Elizabeth scooped another olive from the bowl.

"They're good," she said looking at me, "but not as good as the fire-roasted ones Ron bought for me."

"Food," Rachel once said to me, "is a way to know people better—what food they bring to a potluck, what they eat, what they don't eat. Eating together is an intimate experience. You eat with your friends; you don't eat with strangers."

Her words rang true to me. Certainly when my neighbors and I began eating together on Monday nights, we hardly knew each other. But with each plate of food that passed between us, we moved from being strangers, to acquaintances, to friends.

Joy and Sorrow

*N*ourished by so much food and so many conversations, an actual community of neighbors was taking shape. We were becoming more than the dictionary definition of *neighborhood*—a part of a town or city where people lived. We were also becoming more than the dictionary definition of *neighbors*—people situated near or very near to one another.

We were becoming a community. Brian often described it to new people as a place where he felt belonging, welcome, even love. Of course, not everyone shared his perspective. Certain people enjoyed everyone; for others, just sitting in the same room for any length of time with a particular person required more patience than they could muster. Our relationships ran the gamut from passion to annoyance, from silence to static. In the early years there was a great deal of movement among us—people drifted in and out, some left for months, even years at a time. Sometimes we'd hear from them or they'd come back for a visit. Sometimes we knew they were gone forever.

When I look back on the first few years of becoming friends with my neighbors, it feels like the early days of a love affair, that short and intense period when you can't get enough of the other, when you are desperate to discover all there is in the person who has so absorbed your attention. This wanes, of course. It's impossible—and not particularly healthy—to try to sustain such a manic level of activity. But in the moment, it's exhilarating. You don't even really notice what's happening until much later, when you look back and realize things have slowed into a more reasonable routine. You get more sleep.

In the first three years of connecting with my neighbors, before the inevitable fractures and breaks fully set in, I spent a lot of time with my new friends, sometimes in groups ranging from five to fifteen people, sometimes with just two or three.

Our group activities were so much fun: bocce ball, croquet, and a picnic for Canada Day on the expanse of lawn between our condo and Lake Ontario; another picnic and swim at the small rocky beach near us for Labor Day; Croatian night in Rachel's apartment, when Nicolai brought his whole family to meet us, each of them carrying into the room platters of rice and vegetables, salty cheese, and cured meats—everything made by them earlier that day. Ron and Anna hosted barbecues on their twenty-fifth-floor balcony, where we watched the Toronto Air Show without anything impeding our view; groups of us celebrated birthday parties at clubs like the Lula Lounge and Urban Cowboy, where we laughed more than anything as we learned to salsa and line dance. For a couple of years, Rachel and I hosted Arts and Applause, a grand party that brought our work colleagues, family members, and neighbors together to meet each other. Sixty people showed up, some performing songs, telling stories, or displaying their art, everyone else applauding.

But Christmas in Pajamas was by far my favorite of our communal gatherings.

Up until I moved to Toronto, spending Christmas with various family members seemed my lot as a single woman, and it wasn't a bad one. But, as generous as my siblings were in inviting me to their homes for the holidays, I never felt like I was experiencing Christmas the way I wanted to. While I appreciated their willingness to enfold me in their Christmas traditions, I felt like something was off, like it wasn't quite what I wanted my Christmas to be. Their traditions and their friends weren't mine.

And so, in my second December in Toronto, Rachel and I ushered in a new tradition. On Christmas morning, I rose at 6:30 a.m., slid two cheese frittatas in the oven and fried up a rasher of bacon. By 8 a.m., all was ready, and I opened the door to my apartment. One by one, my neighbors arrived, all, like me, still wearing their pajamas and slippers, all bearing something in their hands to contribute to breakfast—a bowl of batter and whipped cream for Belgian waffles; bottles of orange juice and champagne; a carafe of coffee; platters of strawberries, blueberries, and raspberries.

The second year we celebrated Christmas in Pajamas, Fran was just one month into recovering from hip replacement surgery. Still, she rolled her walker down the hallway, a coffee cake balanced on its seat. She compromised on the dress code, wearing pajama bottoms topped with a festive sweater and a sparkling necklace. Her blonde hair was perfectly coiffed and she was wearing lipstick.

Everyone admired how put together Fran looked, considering her recent surgery and the early morning hour. I suspect the rest of us subconsciously tried to tame down our own unruly hair, just to feel a bit more presentable in her presence. We were all so glad to see her, so relieved she seemed to be recovering so quickly.

I only saw Fran one more time after that, on New Year's Day when Elizabeth and I brought her a bouquet of flowers. While she invited us into her apartment, it was obvious she wasn't really in the mood for company, so we didn't stay long.

Three weeks later she was gone.

"I have really terrible news," Anna's voice on the other end of the phone was serious. "Fran died this week. It was sudden. In her apartment." I listened, speechless, as Anna told me how a mutual Facebook friend had reached out to her. Fran had lots of friends, and Facebook was one avenue where many of us intersected. As soon as I arrived home from work, I texted Elizabeth.

"Are you home? I need to drop by for a moment." I wanted Elizabeth, who had known Fran the longest, to hear the news from me, not Facebook.

Later that evening, a group of us gathered for Monday night dinner at Rachel's apartment and raised our glasses in a somber toast to our neighbor and friend. Then we began retelling the stories Fran had told us—the best one featuring a weekend when, as a teenager, she'd hung out with a legendary folk-rock musician. Fran made our collective jaws drop as she told her story, holding us in suspense for more than an hour, refusing to tell us the name of the celebrity who invited her to dinner because he appreciated her fan letter. We finally coaxed the name out of her and then spent the evening singing snippets of our favorite Gordon Lightfoot tunes—"Sundown," "The Wreck of the Edmund Fitzgerald," and "If You Could Read My Mind."

We all wished we could have read Fran's mind in those last days of her life. But even if we had been able to, it would not have made any difference.

Fran was alone in her apartment when she died, and it was several days before anyone figured out why she wasn't answering calls. We took some solace that her death, likely caused by an aneurism, had been immediate. She probably didn't even have a chance to think about calling anyone for help. We hoped she had not suffered.

I prayed that in the months before her death she had found the peace she once told me she was seeking. The topic had surfaced easily one Monday night as we sat next to each other in Rachel's living room. I had made a passing comment about my church, and Fran picked up on it, asking, "You go to church? Can I go with you sometime?"

"Of course," I replied.

Fran came to church with me a couple of times. "I feel more peaceful after I sit in church," she said as we left the building and headed toward home. Later, she told me she'd returned to the Greek Orthodox church of her childhood, following her roots to see where that would lead. We never had a chance to talk about what she'd discovered.

"I can't get over how empty the building feels without Fran," I said to Elizabeth one Saturday morning as I sat on the small couch in her living room. Across the room, Elizabeth was standing behind the kitchen counter making tiny turkey burgers to freeze for future meals. I'd carried my coffee mug to her place, padding along the short distance between our two apartments in my slippers. Lazily, I propped my feet on her glass coffee table and looked away from her, out through the sliding glass doors, past her balcony. Snow squalls were blowing across the lake. It was a grey day, a good one to be inside drinking coffee with a friend.

"Maybe not so empty," Elizabeth grinned in response.

"What do you mean?" I asked, turning toward her.

"So, last night something weird happened. A pair of my running shoes got moved. I swear it was Fran!"

"You must have moved them and just forgotten about it," I said.

"Nope. I always put those shoes in exactly the same place every time I take them off."

Elizabeth was a creature of habit; I didn't doubt that part of the story. I peered across the room at the small pile of shoes in a jumbled heap across from her kitchen.

"And you think you can tell something was moved in that pile?" I laughed.

"I know my own mess," she said, then, wiping her hands on a cloth, walked the two steps to the pile of shoes and picked up a pair with purple stripes. "I put them here," she said, pointing to a spot on the floor. "And when I got up this morning, they were over here." She pointed to a spot near her front door. "I'm sure Fran moved them. I think she's trying to make me feel better. She was a joker you know. She always liked to play little tricks on people."

"Well, that's true," I said. "But why does she need to make you feel better?"

"I really regret not insisting that Fran let me check in on her daily after her surgery. When we saw her on New Year's Day and she told us she was tired of people checking up on her, that she just wanted to be on her own, I shouldn't have listened. I get the independence. I'm like that too. But now I regret that I didn't check in with her more."

A few days later, Elizabeth had texted Fran from a pizza shop to see if she needed supper. When she didn't get a reply, Elizabeth figured Fran just didn't want to bother anyone.

"After what she'd said to us, I decided to let it go, to not follow up," said Elizabeth. "I know she probably died at night and I couldn't have done anything about that. But maybe I could have let her family know something was wrong sooner.

"Fran's death has taught me two things," Elizabeth continued as she put down the sneakers, returned to the kitchen, and washed her hands under the faucet. "One is to appreciate the people who are here. The other is, even when someone is not well and they say don't check on me, don't support me, I'll do it anyway."

Elizabeth slid the tray of burgers into the oven and set the timer. Carrying her coffee cup across the room, she sat cross-legged in a black leather chair in front of the sliding window. Behind her, the snow swirled. I pulled a blanket from the back of the couch and tucked it around my knees. Elizabeth took a sip of her coffee, then set her cup down and gathered her hair against the nape of her neck, playing with it for a few moments. Finally settled, she spoke again.

"This week, I saw the coroner's van parked outside the building. Later, I ran into the building manager, and I asked him if someone had died. He said, 'Oh yeah, people die in this building every day.' He talked about it in a very cavalier way. He was probably exaggerating, but it got me thinking about Fran again, and how we need to be more aware of each other.

"I grew up engaging with neighbors on my street like they were a second family. When I moved here ten years ago, I began to get to know people who parked near me or were on the same schedule. We'd chat a bit when we'd meet in the parking garage or hallway. I always thought it was weird that I wasn't engaging more with my neighbors here. But the last five years have been different, with all the time we've spent together, all the meals and other things we've done."

Elizabeth and I continued talking; acknowledging that what had happened to Fran could happen to any one of us who lived alone. Although we were in and out of each other's lives a lot, days or even weeks might pass without a connection. Before Fran's death, we simply thought we were respecting each other's right to privacy, valuing our independence. After her death, such thinking seemed foolish. Fran taught us a valuable lesson, and we agreed to check in with each other more often.

Elizabeth, who knew Fran the best, led the way. "If you haven't received a response from me within a day, don't hesitate to break down my door," she declared to Rachel and me one Friday night when the three of us were together in my apartment. Then she handed me an envelope containing the key to her apartment and a list of phone numbers for her parents and brothers.

Such was Fran's parting gift to us. She'd also given me another gift on the last Christmas morning we spent together: one of her black-and-silver studded chokers. It's not really my style, and I'll likely never wear it, but I can't bring myself to give it away. I keep it as a memento of my brief friendship with a bright and beautiful woman. It reminds me that life can be over in an instant. Fran taught me to take better care of people.

And although, unlike Elizabeth, I'm not one to believe in the mischievous presence of a person's spirit, I keep an eye on that necklace. If Fran ever decides to move it, I don't want to miss the joke.

My neighbors and I rarely exchanged material gifts, preferring consumables that require only temporary storage. Even on Christmas Day, if we gave each other anything, it was usually a small, usable token—my homemade grape jelly, Elizabeth's gingersnap cookies, Turkish coffee Brian purchased on his travels, Rachel's hand-designed note cards. One year, the ever-practical Yolanda gave us all light bulbs. Another year she brought a plastic bag stuffed with hundreds of bay leaves, enough for ten years' worth of spaghetti sauce. She'd found them on sale at a local market and couldn't resist buying them all.

Christmas in Pajamas became a tradition for many of my friends. Even when Ron and Anna moved away from Toronto, they made a point of returning in December, partly to spend a few days with their son, but also so they could be with the rest of us. When Brian moved downtown, he'd get himself up early and drive twenty minutes back to our neighborhood. Another friend, who lived further away in his own house, would arrive fully dressed and change into his pajamas once he arrived at my place.

By 11:30 a.m., most people had said their good-byes. I'd tidy up the kitchen and head to my brother's home fifteen minutes down the highway to join in his family's traditions and share their turkey dinner. Having finally figured out what I wanted for my own Christmas tradition, I could more fully relax into my siblings' hospitality. Christmas didn't seem so lonely to me anymore.

Loneliness, in our twenty-first-century society, has become a permanent state for more and more people. In both Canada and the United States, polls reveal that between 40 and 50 percent of people spend more time alone than they want to. They wish they had someone to talk to regularly—but they don't. Resigned to technological connections, they describe instant messaging, video calls, and social media as "better than nothing."

And the problem isn't limited to North America. A couple of years ago, Britain appointed its first Minister of Loneliness. It was needed, former Prime Minister Theresa May said, to respond to the sad reality of modern life.

Author Jake Meador sounds a similar alarm, suggesting we are fast losing the "very notion of community." It is a crisis, he says, "a comprehensive social breakdown that leaves no corner of life untouched, no person immune to its effects."[1]

I enjoy my own company, have dozens of true friends, a family that loves me, and a faith in God that helps me make sense of life in a way that has led to contentment. But I still have experienced enough bouts of loneliness to never wish it on anyone long term.

Loneliness casts a long shadow that touches everyone—people who are part of a couple, live with a family, or live among a community of friends. It is no respecter of age. I remember feeling intensely lonely when I was about five or six, tucked in my bed, with my family within reach. But I couldn't fall sleep, and when my mother asked why, the only answer I could come up with was, "I'm lonely."

Rachel and I once had a conversation about whether the supernatural relationship between a human and God is enough, whether it will fully satisfy our many needs, loneliness included. Perhaps we were asking the wrong question. Perhaps a better question would have been this: Why did God create humans as relational beings? What do we lose when we lose relationship?

In an age of increasing social isolation and epidemic loneliness, it would seem God's command to love our neighbors as
we love ourselves is more crucial than ever. Humans were made
for relationship with God, and we were also made for relationships with each other. Loss and loneliness are inevitable, ripping
one's heart apart. The love of a good neighbor is one way God
stitches it back together.

Love and Loneliness

*O*nce, when Elizabeth and I were talking about the evolution of community, she observed that relationships require two streams of activity. "You have to do individual things, but doing things in a group will determine if you want to spend time one on one."

The problem, of course, is that once people in the group begin spending time in twos or threes, others may feel excluded. It's an unavoidable reality that unleashes both happiness and pain.

Often on Saturdays, Anna and I would head off together, catching the streetcar outside our building to explore the city. For two dollars, we'd join a group of strangers on walks well beyond our neighborhood where we'd learn the history of iconic buildings or discover back alleys made brilliant by graffiti. Rachel, Tanya, and Elizabeth went for runs along the lake early on Sunday mornings. Sometimes I'd join them for the run, but mostly I'd meet them later for coffee. Anna and Fran liked to browse the boutiques on Queen West, then sit for a couple of hours at a bar for an afternoon beer or cocktail.

One summer evening, Yolanda and I went to an outdoor concert in downtown Toronto. That night we danced for hours as a Chilean band sent their rhythms rippling through our bodies and into the lake behind us.

Brian booked dates with Yolanda, Rachel, or me, inviting us individually to dinner, the theater, even the occasional rave (I wasn't courageous enough to say yes to that). Occasionally, when Elizabeth wanted a break from calorie counting, she and Rachel went in search of the perfect eggs benedict. More frequently, I'd receive a Saturday morning text from Elizabeth: "Got any coffee? I'm coming over."

I loved that this was happening, that we were becoming a matrix of friends who sought each other out rather than settling only for organized group events.

I loved it except when I felt excluded—then the small space of my condo would become large with loneliness.

Yolanda loved to linger after everyone else vacated Rachel's apartment on Monday evenings. She'd participate in our leaving rituals, helping carry plates and glasses across to the raised kitchen counter, handing them to Rachel, who stacked them in her tiny dishwasher. As people headed toward the door Rachel would stop clearing plates and offer to spoon leftovers into containers for whoever was interested. Most people said yes, gratefully accepting the plastic container, or, when she ran out of those, a porcelain bowl full of whatever she'd made for us that evening: vegetarian chili, green curry, chicken soup, mac and cheese. It always amazed me that as often as we sent each other home with leftovers—and we all did it—our bowls and containers would find their way back to the rightful owner. Sometimes I'd have bowls and plates on my counter for weeks until someone noticed and said, "Oh, I was wondering where I'd left that."

As everyone left Rachel's apartment, Yolanda would slip onto a kitchen stool and wave good-bye. Then she'd settle in for another thirty or forty minutes, chatting with Rachel until she was gently shooed out the door.

But when Nicolai began coming to Monday night dinners, Yolanda left with everyone else. To stay would have been to get in the way.

Nicolai quietly lingered, leaning his lanky frame against the kitchen counter. A gentle smile creased his bearded face, and his brown eyes were friendly behind black-rimmed glasses as he said good night to each person. But he made no move to leave. And Rachel, who usually ushered everyone but Yolanda out at curfew, didn't seem to mind at all.

Mostly, I didn't either. We all sensed something romantic was going on, although neither Rachel nor Nicolai ever named their relationship. But when they were in proximity to each other, flash fires flamed between them and the rest of us were like moths fluttering around the edges, unable to avoid the sheer brightness of it all.

Leaving Nicolai behind became the norm, and mostly, I didn't think much about it when I'd leave Rachel's apartment. But one Monday night, I couldn't stop thinking, and at 4 a.m. I was still awake, questions piling up in my mind, damming any hope that I might drift back into dreamland.

Where would it lead, this romance between Rachel and Nicolai? Would she be so consumed by relationship with him that our partnership in loving our neighbors would be over? Would she spend more and more time with him and less with me and our other friends? Why was I so concerned about this? Love is natural. Why couldn't I just be happy for her? Was I jealous?

Rachel and I once sat in a coffee shop together, intent on our own conversation, when a well-dressed man in his fifties approached, told her she was pretty, and offered her his number. This is not an unusual occurrence for Rachel. It has never happened to me.

Observing the interaction between that man and Rachel, I didn't feel jealous. But I did feel invisible. Not seen. Alone, even though I was in the company of my friend, who I knew saw me, enjoyed my company, and was committed to our friendship.

Even so, the 4 a.m. questions hurled themselves at me, I suspect roused less by envy than fear. I was afraid that one of Rachel's romances (and there were a couple more after Nicolai) would end the intentional relationship we shared with each other. From the very beginning, ours was never simply a friendship. Certainly, it was birthed in the normal way of friendships—during that first Starbucks encounter, we realized we liked each other and wanted to get to know each other better. But our friendship mostly flourished because we shared a purpose, a mission. We both wanted to love our neighbors by opening our lives to them and, when invited, step into their lives as well.

When, somewhat embarrassed, I told Rachel about my fear, she assured me that she wasn't going anywhere. If and when she committed to a romantic relationship, it would be with a man who shared her passion for hospitality, who was as committed as she was to welcoming others in ways that made them feel seen, known, received. She was also looking for someone who, as Elizabeth used to quip, "was following the Jesus." The phrase always made us laugh, but we knew that it was true. Rachel wanted someone who was more interested in Jesus than in her.

I knew all this about Rachel. I also knew myself well, and while I'd had seasons in my life when I wanted to be married, mostly I've been content. I rarely feel lonely when I am alone, finding plenty to occupy my time—reading, writing, tending my balcony garden, chopping vegetables for big pots of soup, wandering the paths along the lake, camera in hand and composing photos of cardinals, wrens, and ducks. I happily take myself on long drives, in search of a rural farm market where I'll wander the stalls and inevitably come home with a ten-pound bag of sweet peppers or a bushel of tomatoes, more than a single woman could ever use. In fact, such a thought rarely surfaces because I rarely think of myself as single. I have so many friends—surely they'll want a share of the peppers.

I love solitary road trips because they give me lots of time to think. If I have a writing assignment in front of me, I'll have the whole piece composed by the time I'm headed for home. For a drive like this to be truly satisfying, it needs to be two hours or more; then my mind can settle into whatever issue I am trying to resolve or whatever story I am wanting to tell.

Loneliness rarely surfaces when I am alone. Instead, it tends to prick me when I am with people who share a connection beyond my reach. I was lonely when I spent Christmas with my siblings and their families. I was lonely when I went to weddings and I knew my friends had to figure out where to seat me, the guest without a plus one. I was lonely when I watched good friends move into a new romantic relationship. I was happy for them, but still lonely.

Loneliness punctured my otherwise contented life when Nicolai lingered in Rachel's apartment and I headed down the hall to mine.

I wasn't alone in my loneliness. I think we all felt it at different times and for different reasons. Sometimes we let it get the better of us, not connecting with each other for days or weeks. After Fran's death, we became more aware of the need to connect. But still we slipped back into old habits of independence, forgetting just how precarious that was.

For a long time I never told anyone about my loneliness. I wrote about it in my journal, thought about it on my long drives until eventually the feeling dissipated and I'd be back to my cheerful self. I was unable to tell anyone but myself about my need, but the need was real. I was the one in need of a neighbor's love.

It's easy for someone like me to mask loneliness, even when it's ripping a hole in my heart. I am a practiced optimist, certain things will get better eventually. I'm not just a glass-half-full kind of girl; mostly I feel like my cup is running over. *Don't complain, you've been blessed, lots of people are worse off than you, life is good, you have everything you need.* These have been the mantras of my life.

In the right dosage, they aren't bad mantras. But I'd been over-dosing on them for a long time and had built up a bit of resistance to truth. Over the years, my unfiltered neighbors taught me that a well-placed lament leads to change. Blessings are delightful, but sorrow brings its own gifts. Yes, there are people worse off than me, but that doesn't mean I should ignore the rough patches in my own life. They're real and painful and they shape me whether I admit it or not. And as for having everything I needed? Well, that was a lie I was telling myself. I needed my neighbors just as much as they needed me. Thankfully, they could see that, even when I couldn't.

One Saturday morning, after Bible study had ended and most everyone else had left, Yolanda and Rachel remained. Coffee cups cooled and crumbs littered the plates where earlier there had been chocolate chip banana bread. It was a cold, snowy day, the kind that makes you want to curl up in a blanket. Luka had done just that, tucking himself under a blanket on the futon in my spare bedroom where he watched a movie on his tablet.

"You look really beautiful today." Rachel's words surprised me. I was wearing minimal makeup, a touch of blush on my cheeks, a trace of green eyeliner edging my lower lids.

Yolanda picked up the theme: "I love your style. And those colors really work for you. You are beautiful." Sitting across from the two of them, my legs stretched out, feet taking up space on the coffee table next to the piles of discarded dishes, I looked down at my clothes, a loose, navy blue tunic and an orange tank top, grey leggings, toes painted with bright blue polish. My favorite clothes and jewelry are the ones that bring out my inner Bohemian, but they also serve a more practical purpose. I carry a fat little inner tube around my hips. Tunics hide it nicely.

"You know," I replied. "I never feel beautiful. I'm fat, have crooked teeth, and permanent dark circles under my eyes."

"Are your teeth crooked?" Yolanda leaned across the table toward me for a closer look. "I've never noticed that." I was surprised someone who took such care with her own teeth had never noticed the deficiencies in mine.

"You really don't think you are beautiful? I'm serious. You are!" Rachel was looking at me, shocked. "This needs to change. I'm going to start praying that God changes your view of yourself."

"I'll take all the prayer I can get!" I laughed. And then I never thought about her declaration again until two weeks later when I was taking my car through a car wash on a Saturday afternoon. I was mesmerized by the blasts of sudsy water erasing salty grime when the *whoosh* of my cell phone took my attention from the *whoosh* of water. I looked to see who was texting me.

"Just thinking about you." It was Brian. Smiling, I picked up the phone, grateful for something to do while the five-minute car wash cycled through.

"I wanted to tell you I think you are really pretty."

"Have you been talking to Rachel?" I texted back.

"No, why?"

"Never mind. And thanks!"

"I'm serious. I'm attracted to you in the purest sense of the word. Too bad I'm gay. We could get married."

I was laughing out loud by this point, shaking my head and thinking this would be one car wash I'd never forget. Later that night, I crawled into bed and pulled out my journal. I rarely write in the evening, but some days have gems that need to be recorded. This was such a day.

Brian was full of compliments about me today . . . so remarkable given that Rachel prayed I'd know I am beautiful—and not just on the inside. I rarely feel beautiful. Sometimes I think I look presentable. But pretty? No. I have dark circles under my eyes, pudgy face, crooked teeth. On the other hand, my eyes are big and brown and people react to my smile. My hair falls into style and is shiny. I shall never be vain about my looks but I am receiving these compliments and prayers as gifts.

I closed the journal, snuggled down under the duvet, and turned out my light. That night, I was not troubled by 4 a.m. questions. My friends had seen me—truly seen me—and more than that, they had spoken truth about me so unexpectedly that I was actually able to receive it. I fell asleep as my loneliness drifted far, far away.

Lost and Found

*R*achel and Nicolai's romance lasted about eight months. When they decided it would be best not to see each other at all, Nicolai stopped coming to Monday night dinners, Bible study, and Writers' Group.

But for more than a year afterward, Nicolai and I stayed in touch.

In spite of the difference in our ages—I was old enough to be his mother—we'd become friends. Even while he and Rachel were seeing each other, he and I spent time together without her. Sometimes we'd have long conversations about religion or philosophy at our neighborhood coffee shop; at other times we'd meet at a local pub and listen to a live blues band over dinner. I introduced him to a couple of friends of mine who also loved to study the Bible, and for several months Nicolai and I joined them every Tuesday night for dinner at their house where we would engage in a thoughtful discussion based on the Gospel of Matthew.

Throughout my life, I've had friendships with lots of people younger than me, appreciating the privilege of walking with them as they figure out who they are and what matters in life. It's been the focus of my work and volunteer life for more than forty years.

But my friendship with Nicolai was different. I became friends with Nicolai because he was my neighbor. I sometimes wondered if his continued friendship with me after the breakup with Rachel was pragmatic on his part—he never ceased to inquire about her or ask me to pass on his greetings. But, ultimately, I knew our friendship was also our own. When he returned from a trip to Croatia, long after he and Rachel broke up, he brought me a small clay candle-holder as a gift. And long before that, he gave me the gift of an extraordinary evening when we let music lead our conversation.

Nicolai knocked on my door promptly at 7 p.m. I opened the door, standing to one side as he made his way into the small entryway, navigating the space with the added bulk of a guitar case.

"How are you?" he asked, setting the case in a corner and giving me a hug.

"I'm great," I replied. "It's Friday night, the work week is done, and we're going to make some music!"

That evening is one of my favorite memories of time spent with Nicolai. Discovering he liked to play the guitar, I'd told him I liked to sing, which resulted in us planning a Friday night jam session at my apartment. We'd invited other friends to join us, but they all declined.

Settling himself on one side of my couch, Nicolai began quietly strumming, picking out notes as I listened. This went on for a while, him playing, me guessing the tune, but too nervous to break into song.

"It feels a little awkward, doesn't it?" I finally confessed, readjusting my position several times as I sat kitty-corner to him, the coffee table between us. Nicolai nodded, but continued playing.

"Well, let's get over it," I said, finally, and then stopped talking and began to sing. We worked our way through many songs that night: Leonard Cohen's "Hallelujah," Paul Simon's "Graceland," and Simon and Garfunkel's "Scarborough Fair." Every song led us down new conversational paths. As he played more Cohen, I pulled out my copy of *Beautiful Losers* and leafed through its pages, reading snatches of his poetic prose. But when Nicolai began playing "Scarborough Fair," I held up my hand.

"Wait, I'm not sure I can sing that."

"Why not?" Nicolai looked surprised.

And so, I told him about my one and only experience in a strip club nearly forty years earlier during my second year of university. On that night, I watched a woman wrap her body around a pole, the melody of "Scarborough Fair" plaintive in the background. I was in a small town where the same patrons watched the same show night after night. The woman performed, but no one applauded, no one actually seemed to appreciate her at all. I think that bothered me as much the selling of her body for cash. I never could hear the song again without remembering the woman and how alone, how unseen, she seemed.

"Well," Nicolai said, balancing the guitar on his knee and looking at me with his steady, thoughtful gaze, "I think we should sing it anyway." And he began, a little tentatively, moving slowly through the phrases: "Are you going to Scarborough Fair, Parsley . . ." he looked at me, smiling encouragingly " . . . rosemary . . . and thyme." Finally, I paired my voice with his.

"Remember me to one who lived there. She was once a true love of mine." We finished the song, redeeming it together.

A couple of hours into our jam session, Rachel, Brian, and Elizabeth showed up, and Nicolai put his guitar away. I opened a bottle of wine and set crackers and cheese out on my coffee table.

"So, how was the song session?" Rachel asked.

"Pretty awkward," I laughed.

"Hey, we were good," protested Nicolai.

As Nicolai and I made room for our friends to sit with us, our conversation turned to the trust we could sense was growing among us. Brian summed it up best, observing we'd grown to know each other in a short time because we'd intentionally been spending time together, choosing to talk with each other openly, to be transparent and vulnerable.

"But you know," he continued, "we should never let our friendship with each other be a barrier to new people we might meet. We should always be ready to welcome new people in.

"When I'm with you guys, it's fun. I feel warmth, I feel belonging. But I know you have lives. I know it's fleeting. We get together for a meal, watch a movie, spend two or three hours together. But then it's gone. And you're waiting for the next time."

And the next time may or may not come. Fran taught us that.

Her death meant she would only ever come back to us in memories. Shortly after she died, a few of us attended a party in honor of her sixty-fifth birthday. It was held at a local bar, the place Fran had once described to me as her church because that's where she met her friends every Sunday afternoon.

We needed to let people go, to release them from being neighbors to being something else. Fran became a memory. By the time Anna and Ron left Toronto and when Brian eventually bought a downtown condo and moved out of our building, we'd all become good friends. With Anna and Ron, and with Brian, I knew we'd always be able to dive back into each other's lives regardless of how much time had passed without us seeing each other. But Nicolai slowly drifted away, only showing up in my life every now and then by his choice, not mine.

The more time I spent with my neighbors, the more I began to love them—and their pets, too. Even Brian's parrot, who mostly annoyed me, had something to teach me about loving my neighbors.

"Jewel's disappeared. I'm going out to help Brian hunt for her." Rachel's text sliced into my quiet summer evening. I'd been eating dinner on my balcony and had just stepped inside to carry my dishes to the kitchen counter when I noticed the message flashing on my cell phone screen.

"Oh no!" I texted back. "Where are you?"

"Just across the street—near the ramp to the highway."

"I'll be there in a few minutes to help." I sent the message then quickly pulled on long pants, socks, and sneakers. It was a hot evening, but I didn't want to be wandering around long grass in bare legs. Truthfully, I was not thrilled by the idea of searching through the hardscrabble landscape bordering the highway ramp. It was a sizeable wasteland, shaped like a quarter of a pie (but far less appetizing) with lots of garbage strewn among the brambles. I tried not to think about what I might stumble upon in the undergrowth, but images of snakes and rats scurried around the edges of my mind.

I went, though, because I knew how important Jewel was to Brian—the two had been together for twelve years. Losing the parrot would be devastating to him. I locked my door, tucked my keys in my pocket, and headed toward the wasteland.

As I crossed the street, I could see Rachel walking slowly along the edge of the highway ramp. There was no sidewalk, just a bank of long grass, thorny wild rosebushes, and masses of dandelions. Brian had jumped the chain link fence that surrounded the land housing a shuttered factory. I could hear the squeak of a toy he often used to entertain Jewel. Heading in the opposite direction, I ventured into the dreaded vacant lot.

"Jewel, where are you?" I yelled, wondering how I would ever spot her emerald feathers against masses of green leaves. Gnarly twigs and brambles snatched at my legs as I waded through the undergrowth, and I kept my eyes peeled on the ground around me, looking for Jewel but also for holes and anything that might live in them. I did not want to trip and fall. I wandered nervously around the scrubby land, half expecting to find someone's makeshift home set up in one of its wooded corners. I was keenly aware that humans, snakes, raccoons, and rats probably frequented the area. There were bottles, cans, plastic bags, and food wrappers everywhere. Every now and then I'd sense a flickering in the trees, but it was always a small songbird, never Jewel.

Our voices rang out, mixed with the sounds of traffic. "Jewel, where are you? Come home!"

We hunted until dusk, then Rachel and I headed home. Brian had a flashlight and continued hunting in the dark. I was not brave enough to join him, hoping that with his military training he'd be fine on his own.

I went to bed that night sending up prayers that Brian would find Jewel, and if he didn't, that she would be safe through the night. I also prayed that Brian's heart would remain hopeful, that it wouldn't be wracked with guilt. Jewel had flown off his shoulder while the two had been biking—Brian pedaling with the parrot perched on his shoulder. He often took Jewel with him when he went out for a walk or a bike ride. Usually she didn't budge but on this particular evening something had spooked her and she'd flown away from him just as a gust of wind blew across the lake. Brian figured she was caught on the wind's currents and flew further than she usually would have.

At 7:15 the next morning, as Tanya, Rachel, and I were heading toward the lake for an early morning jog, we met Brian at the backdoor of our building. He'd had no success the night before and was heading back out into the wasteland to search for Jewel. We assured him we'd keep our eyes peeled for her as we jogged along the lake.

By eight o'clock, we'd finished our thirty-minute run and were sitting in the sunshine enjoying cups of coffee at our neighborhood café. Perfectly situated on the ground floor of the building in front of mine, the café opens onto a wide sidewalk that extends from the lake to the highway. Suddenly a flash of green whisked by me, flying low along the sidewalk.

"That was Jewel!" I yelled, not concerned about the early morning hour or that I might be disturbing the other patrons sitting around the patio. Rachel and I leapt from our chairs, chasing Jewel and leaving Tanya behind with our wallets and coffee cups.

"You looking for a bird? She flew under that bush," a man standing outside the back door of our building pointed us in the right direction. "If I were you, I'd try to cover her with your jacket then scoop her out from there."

Rachel kneeled and followed his directions, gently laying her sweatshirt over Jewel, who sat quietly, seemingly unscathed and unperturbed by her night out. I texted Brian: "We've found Jewel!"

"This is a miracle," Rachel said as she gathered the bird into her arms. "I can't believe we found her!"

Rachel and I had both prayed fervently for Jewel's safe return, our prayers as motivated as much by our concern for Brian as for the parrot. We knew how much he loved her, had watched him stroking her feathers, allowing her beak to peck at his lips. He often held her upside down from his index finger as he caressed the underside of her belly. She would hang there contentedly as if it were the best perch in the world. Jewel was family to Brian, a constant, living presence in his apartment. He worried about keeping her cooped up, which is why he insisted on taking her biking or for walks in the city.

After losing her, even for that one night, he seemed more aware of the constrained life he was imposing on her. His frequent trips out of the city for work left her lonely, and even though several of us checked in on her, she was never satisfied with our company. She took to hiding under the couch in his living room, digging out the stuffing and turning it into a nest. Then she'd find one of her small white toy balls and sit on it, as if it were an egg.

Eventually, Brian found a home for Jewel with a family who kept several parrots. She was happier there, he said. I agreed, even though I missed her at our dinners and parties. I'd gotten used to the feel of her claws at the back of my neck as she walked from one shoulder to the other. I'd long forgiven her for the sticky splotches she dropped on my floor and windowsills.

When she lived near me, I could not help but be aware of her, and even more than that, to be interested and concerned for her. She made me smile with her antics, playing her own form of soccer with her white balls when she wasn't trying to hatch them. When it was my turn to check on her, I was always relieved when I'd open the door to Brian's apartment and hear her squawk. I was less impressed when, after sitting with her for a while, I'd take my leave, only to hear her scream in anger as I stood at the elevator beyond Brian's apartment. She knew how to make her point.

In her own way, Jewel was one of my neighbors, just like Brian or Yolanda or Anna and Ron. She lived close enough for me to see her, both at random moments and by design. She made my life more interesting and purposeful—I enjoyed meeting her needs when Brian was away. Jewel needed people to feed and water her. And she needed company. She needed the people who lived in proximity to her to pay attention, to be aware of her, to be involved in her life.

And then, when Brian moved her on to a new home, she no longer had any need of us at all.

But I haven't forgotten her. We spent too much time with her for that.

Like all the neighbors, Jewel contributed to my understanding of why loving one's neighbors makes sense, why it is a good and worthwhile practice.

There's nothing contractual in a neighborly relationship. It's not like marriage or adoption. Nor is there a blood connection that suggests lifelong familial responsibility. Rather, neighbor relationships are about the here and now, about the people who are around you at a given moment.

There is a spectrum of choices available to us as we consider the people who live in proximity to us. At one end is the option to ignore. At the other is the option to love. In between we can choose to acknowledge, tolerate, to appreciate and like, to enjoy. We can also choose to ignore, disregard, dismiss, dislike, and even to hate.

Loving is perhaps the hardest choice, in part because the very nature of a neighborhood, especially these days, is marked by transience. We are a society of movement. People—and parrots—don't stick around for a long time.

I mourned when Nicolai drifted out of my life. Unlike with Brian or Ron and Anna, I didn't know if we would ever pick up the threads of friendship. And when Yolanda announced she and Luka were moving halfway around the world, I feared I would lose them, too. After all, she never wanted to pronounce us friends. Why would acquaintances bother to stay in touch?

Beyond Acquaintances

I'd never even heard of the Republic of Kiribati until Yolanda announced at a dinner one Monday night that she and Luka were planning to move there. We'd been gathering for a couple of years by this time—nearly one hundred meals and a good many stories had knitted us together whether we admitted it or not.

"We're going for two years," she told the group of us gathered for dinner at Rachel's, and then added with a provocative grin, "or maybe forever."

None of us had actually heard of Kiribati, a spattering of mostly uninhabited islands in the South Pacific Ocean. Yolanda and Luka were heading for Abaiang, not even an island, really, but a coral reef formed around a lagoon. Abaiang, Yolanda told us, had a population of about 5,500 people living on sixteen kilometers of land. She would be teaching at a boarding school run by a Catholic mission, which she'd found online as she searched for travel options.

Excitedly, she told us about the volunteer opportunity she'd applied for as an English teacher to junior and senior high school students. The mission would pay her way to Kiribati and provide living accommodations in return for her teaching skills.

I wasn't completely surprised by Yolanda's plans, but neither was I convinced she would follow through. More and more through the past year, she'd been declaring her intention to move away.

The week after her dinner announcement, Yolanda called me at work. She rarely used her phone, so I answered the call, wondering what was up.

"I have a favor to ask," she said. "Would you provide a reference for me?"

"Of course," I replied, realizing Yolanda's plans were becoming more concrete. Perhaps this was really going to happen. Perhaps she really was going to leave.

Over the next few months, she found someone to rent her apartment, moved most of her personal belongings into Brian's storage locker, sent Luka's gecko to live with his father, and canceled the insurance on her car. Three weeks before they were scheduled to leave, she had another favor to ask of me.

"Would you mind if Luka and I stayed with you for a couple of weeks?" The date of her leaving had been pushed back several times by the mission organization and a tenant was ready to move into her apartment. I said yes immediately but wondered what I might be getting myself into. On the day Yolanda and Luka were to move in, I was up early in the morning, reading Scripture, praying and reflecting on the days ahead. I wrote in my journal:

Yolanda and Luka move in with me today and will be here until they leave for Kiribati. She asked if they could stay and I had no good reason to say no. They are my friends. They need a place to stay. Yolanda is unpredictable these days, tense because of the move. But even so . . .

Yolanda and Luka turned out to be the perfect houseguests. Luka was his usual quiet and polite self, and Yolanda worked out her tension by cleaning—it was her pattern in her own apartment and she could not avoid it in mine. I'm a casual host, asking guests to make themselves at home, take what they want from the fridge and cupboards. I cleaned the house before she moved in but warned Yolanda not to look too closely in the corners. I'm not a perfectionist when it comes to housekeeping, or anything else for that matter.

I was away on the final week of their visit and by the time I returned, Yolanda and Luka had moved out, choosing to stay with his father for their last couple of nights in Toronto. As I went from room to room, I discovered evidence of Yolanda everywhere. My bathroom mirrors sparkled. The corners of the laundry cupboard that housed my washer and dryer were spotless—usually they were sticky with lint and dribbles of laundry detergent. I am an out-of-sight, out-of-mind housekeeper; Yolanda was the opposite, cleaning every nook and cranny. I imagined her down on her knees, wielding a toothbrush. When I opened the refrigerator, I discovered not only had she cleaned it, she'd organized it, lining jam jars and preserves on the top shelf, placing yogurt, milk, and eggs tidily in the middle. Along the door, bottles of ketchup, mustard, pickles, and soy sauce were lined up like soldiers. She'd also left me a few things from her cupboards—a massive jar of sauerkraut, a restaurant-size bag of dried cranberries, a couple bottles of honey, and eight packages of dried seaweed. Yolanda's bargain hunting would serve me even when she was on the other side of the equator.

"Why Kiribati?" I asked Yolanda one evening while she was living with me. Thanks to yet another power outage, we were sitting in the dark with a candle glowing between us on the coffee table. We agreed the setting was appropriate—it would be the third time we'd sat in the darkness together over the course of our three-year friendship. As I'd discovered with Elizabeth, there was something about shared powerlessness that encouraged openness between us.

The first power outage Yolanda and I experienced together had been on a Monday night when I was hosting dinner. That night, torrential rain had fallen across the city for three hours, causing havoc with supper-time traffic and shutting down subways and tramlines. A few of my neighbors made their way home from work by sloshing miles through knee-high water. Once home, rather than sit, damp and discouraged, in their own apartments they climbed the stairs to my place, bringing food to share so it wouldn't spoil. That night we feasted on salads, hummus, watermelon, and lots of ice cream.

Thanks to Yolanda's spontaneous nature, the second power outage we shared included Luka. It was a wintery night and, almost ready to go to bed, I was dressed in a floor-length white flannel nightdress, the top pleated and embroidered with red thread. Responding to a quiet knock on my door, I peered through the peephole and saw Yolanda and Luka standing in the hallway. I opened the door and my arms to them.

"Your nightdress!" Yolanda exclaimed as she took in my appearance. "It reminds me of a story from Ukraine's history. Can we come in for a visit? Luka and I didn't want to sit at home in the dark." One of the benefits of living in a vertical neighborhood is you can easily visit each other regardless of the obstacles weather throws at you. If you don't mind climbing steps when the elevators shut down, you never need to be alone on a stormy night.

"Come in. Tell me the story," I said and Yolanda, never one to turn down an offer to talk about Ukraine, happily obliged. Luka snuggled up beside his mother on one end of the couch, and I sat on another as she told us both the story dating back to the First World War when Russians invading a Ukrainian village mistook the villagers' long, white, embroidered night dresses for ball gowns. Wives of the Russian officers wore them to a fancy ball, much to the humor of the Ukrainian villagers who didn't have much else to laugh about.

Yolanda was proud of Ukraine but for all her love of travel, she never seemed to want to return permanently to the country she'd left at age twenty. In fact, on the night of our third shared power outage, when she was living with me in advance of moving, Yolanda told me that when she was a teenager she wanted to run away, not just from her home in Ukraine, but from her life.

And then I began to understand the answer to my question: "Why Kiribati?"

On the night of our third power outage, we sat across from each other on my couch, a bottle of wine opened between us as we feasted on crackers, cheese, and a bowl of Yolanda's homemade cucumber and dill salad. I listened as Yolanda told me yet another story.

"When I was in high school, we read Somerset Maugham's book—I don't know the title in English, only in Ukraine. But I think it has something about the moon . . . and perhaps the word *pence* is in it."

I picked up my cell phone and Googled the words moon, pence, and Maugham.

"*The Moon and Sixpence?*" I asked.

"Yes, that's it," replied Yolanda. "It is about a man who is a rich aristocrat, married, part of the elite. He picks up and goes to live in Polynesia, or perhaps the Caribbean. I don't remember exactly. And he begins to be a painter and make babies with tribal women. I remember I was indignant. I was livid. This was only a character in a book, but I owned the situation as if it happened in real life. I remember thinking only men get to act like this. What gives them permission? How do they give themselves permission to behave the way they behave? I told myself I would do something very outrageous. Evolutionary. Against social expectations, what is expected of me.

"And then I did nothing. I totally complied. I felt like I was a sellout because I settled and settled and settled."

Yolanda paused briefly to take a sip of wine. I knew I did not need to ask her any questions, to prompt her to continue. Given an audience, Yolanda would always perform. She continued:

"I am not a rebel anymore. Everything is a calculated risk for me. It took me being mindful of my finances to push myself now. I can still pull some money out of my savings. Luka is the right age, not yet old enough for university. This is a great opportunity for Luka. It's two years of our lives. I don't know what will happen after that. But I am buying myself two years."

She picked up a knife and sliced into a wedge of Gouda, chewing slowly. I held my wine glass, watching the candlelight reflect against it, thinking we had our similarities, Yolanda and I. We were both opportunists. My father once gave me the advice to take every opportunity that came my way. And I've heeded it, saying yes to jobs, even when they meant moving from small-town New Brunswick to big-city Toronto. I've never regretted any of those decisions.

But I usually felt like I was moving toward something new, not trying to escape something old. Only once had I seized an opportunity because I wanted to run away—in that case I knew I needed to leave a job at a newspaper where nobody seemed to really care about the quality of the work. I was twenty-seven years old and shocked by the malaise of the place. I stayed in the job nine months, often coming home and flopping on the living room couch, not bothering to turn on the lights or prepare supper. All I could do was sit there, crying with frustration and anger. When a former colleague called out of the blue and offered me a new job in a new city, I said yes immediately.

But that was my exception. Generally, I am content with my life until it ceases to challenge me. And then, poised for change, I begin to seek the next thing, always looking for a solid and secure place to land.

This was not Yolanda's way. She continued her story.

"Ever since I was sixteen, I have had this persistent thought that I was going to run away and escape. That was always because of Maugham. I don't know why Kiribati, but I was very specific when

I sent in my volunteer application. That's where I wanted to go. Maybe because it is warm there."

I admired her courage, her determination to chase a long-held dream into reality. Later, after she and Luka had moved away, I read *The Moon and Sixpence*, stopping to ponder a question the narrator poses, realizing it helped me understand Yolanda a little better and, perhaps, myself as well.

> Is to do what you most want, to live under the conditions that please you, in peace with yourself, to make a hash of life? . . . I suppose it depends on what meaning you attach to life, the claim which you acknowledge to society, and the claim of the individual.[1]

But before she left, as we sat together in darkness, I had more questions than understanding.

"Will you miss life here?" I asked.

Yolanda looked across the coffee table at me. The apartment was quiet, the kind of stillness that only comes when the electricity has been shut off, when the white noise we live with every day without even noticing dissipates into the darkness. It was so quiet, I think I would have heard the slither of a lie should Yolanda have chosen to be less than transparent. But that was never Yolanda's way. With her, you could always be certain that what she was saying was exactly what she believed. At least, in that moment.

"Right now, I am already missing the community. You have my absolute truthful answer. But once I find myself in Kiribati, I will prohibit myself to dwell on it."

I didn't doubt her. But then, on that gentle night, neither of us had any idea of what she and Luka would face in Kiribati or how much she would need her friends back home to make it through.

Less than a month later, I received a short and urgent email: "I am asking for prayer." Attached to the email, was a longer message

Yolanda had sent to the director of the mission. Life on the tiny Pacific island was not going smoothly. Her legs, bitten by mosquitoes, were badly infected and swollen to nearly three times their usual size. She was in so much pain she had to teach her classes sitting down. The small medical clinic on the island was closed, seas were too rough for boats, and winds too forceful for planes to land. Prayer and rest seemed her only options for healing. Rachel and I prayed. Rachel's mom and aunties prayed. I asked the people in my church to pray.

Eventually we received news that she was better. We breathed a collective sigh of relief. And then, about a month later, another plea for prayer arrived by email.

> Yet again, asking for a prayer, for Luka this time—third day he is running a fever with no other symptoms.

A day or so later, Yolanda and I managed one of our infrequent Skype calls. She would sit in the computer lab at her school, her students walking by from time to time peering over her shoulder at the screen. I would sit in my living room, holding my iPad in my lap, relieved to be seeing and talking to her face-to-face. The connection was never strong on her end, and we'd often have to reconnect several times. But on that night, we talked for about thirty minutes. In spite of its challenges, Yolanda and Luka loved life in Kiribati. Their small house overlooked a white sand beach and aqua seas. Luka was learning to spear fish and climb trees in search of coconuts; they were both scuba diving. We signed off that night and I trusted everything would be well.

But then, a new email arrived titled, "Fourth bad day for Luka."

> My boy is burning up—he is also taking antibiotics just in case, but we still don't know the cause of such high temperature he is having for the fourth day now.

Another week went by and we heard nothing. No emails, no responses to my Skype calls. We could do nothing but pray, and pray we did. Rachel and I prayed daily, we met weekly to pray with her mom and aunties. I was often awake at 4 a.m., sending desperate prayers heavenward, not even trying to go back to sleep. Finally, one night, I decided I needed to do something more concrete, so I got out of bed and turned on my computer, searching out the contact information for the director of the mission. I was grateful I still had it from when I'd written Yolanda's reference letter.

> I am a friend of Yolanda's back in Canada. I am very sorry to bother you, but I was wondering if you could give me an update on her and Luka. I usually hear from Yolanda every day or two, but it has been more than a week now. The last time I heard from her, Luka was quite sick, and she was considering taking him to the hospital on another island. It is unusual to have no news from her for so many days, and I have become increasingly concerned. They are dear friends and an important part of my community. It would be helpful to know what is going on, if at all possible. Even knowing they did go to the hospital would help calm my worries and help me to know how to pray for them.

The next day I received a welcome, although infuriatingly short response. "They are back and all is well."

A day or so later, Yolanda and I Skyped, and she filled in the details of Luka's illness, a viral infection requiring a week-long stay at the hospital on a nearby island. Their health scares were over, but life on Abaiang never got any easier, even though both Yolanda and Luka loved the landscape, the sun, and the sea. Nine months after they left our neighborhood, they were back. Yolanda had too many concerns for Luka's well-being to remain on the isolated island.

Not long before they returned, we shared a memorable Skype conversation.

"You know how I would always say I was just spending time with all of you for social reasons?" Yolanda asked. "When we would argue about whether we were friends or acquaintances? Well, I think about you all the time."

I smiled into my iPad screen, sending as much love as possible to my neighbor who was so far away but so close to my heart.

"The feeling is mutual," I said to her. "I think about you, and I pray for you a lot. But it's not the same as having you next door."

Yolanda, true to her surprising self, never told us she had decided to come back home. One night she simply walked through the dining room door into Writers' Group, grinning broadly as we all hooted and cheered, pushing back our chairs so we could give her hugs.

I knew things couldn't go back to what they had been before she'd left. No one had heard from Nicolai for more than a year. Ron and Anna had moved back to the United States. Brian had purchased a condo twenty minutes away, and Tanya had moved several streets north of our building. There were new faces around the Writers' Group table, people who had no idea what Yolanda's story was when she walked through the door. But I was thrilled she was back.

The next time she distanced herself from us it wasn't to chase a dream halfway around the world. It was because she was angry at Brian.

Finding Forgiveness

*Y*ou're writing about how we all fell in love. But really, it's more like we're getting divorced."

I let a few seconds pass before I looked at Yolanda, focusing my gaze instead on the calm expanse of Lake Ontario and the sailboats drifting along the horizon. The sun was hot and there was hardly a cloud in the sky. Closer to the shoreline, a swan dipped its head, searching the water for food.

I was searching too. Muddling about in my mind, trying to catch hold of my thoughts as they swam by. I knew there was truth in Yolanda's words, but they weren't the whole story. Of that I was certain. She spoke again before I caught hold of anything worth saying out loud.

"I'm not going to tell you any of the details, and I don't want you to interfere. But I've had it with Brian. It's all over."

"I'm sorry," I said, turning, finally, to look at her. She looked relaxed in spite of the anger roiling beneath her words. Her skin was the color of honey from many days spent like this one. Stretched out on a towel in a red bikini, toes pointed toward the lake, elbows propping up her long, lean body, she'd bundled her blonde hair into a knot on the top of her head, but a few strands had escaped, falling softly around her face.

Shifting my body, I turned toward Yolanda as I stretched out on the blanket, leaning on one arm, and tucking the skirt of my sundress around my knees. I hadn't come to the lake to sunbathe or swim. I'd come to find Yolanda, knowing she'd be drawn to the beach on this unusually hot September day. It was one of her favorite places.

I had just returned from a four-month sabbatical. Although I'd been thousands of miles away from my neighbors, they'd been with me in spirit. I'd taken the time to write the story of our relationships, to set down all that God had been teaching me about why I ought to love my neighbors and to let them love me back.

"I've finished writing the first draft of my book, and I have a copy for you. I'd love you to read it," I said, knowing already what Yolanda's answer would be.

"Thank you, but I've already told you I don't want to read it. When you interviewed me, I gave you permission to put me in the book. You still have it."

"Why don't you want to read it? It would help me make sure I've told the story in a way that people can live with. I don't expect everyone to agree with everything I've written, but your feedback is really important."

"Nobody ever presents me the way I see myself," Yolanda replied. "It's better if I don't read it. I might never read it. But I gave you my permission already to write it. I can live with that."

I knew better than to try to convince her. Eventually, curiosity won out, and she did read early versions of the story I was trying to tell. I was grateful. Yolanda, meticulous in so many ways, sent me texts as she read, pointing out typographical errors and places where my memory had not served me well. But she never pushed back about the way I'd described her. She'd given me permission to write about her and that was enough.

That day on the beach, I knew better than to argue, trusting time would take care of my concern that Yolanda, and all my neighbors, would be at peace with the way I was telling our story. Instead, I let her words drift away and gave my attention to the smooth round stones on the beach. Picking one up, I turned it over in my palm, examined it, then laid it down, choosing another and then another, until finally I found what I was looking for, a rougher stone etched with a tiny fossil. Yolanda had been the first person to show me such treasures were nestled among the shards of builder's concrete used to create the beach on which we sat. Over the years of our friendship she'd given me several as gifts, and I'd added them to the small collection of rocks I keep on my balcony to remind me of other places I've lived and loved.

I handed my treasure to Yolanda who accepted it, her blue eyes keen with curiosity.

"I am sorry about you and Brian," I said looking toward her once more. "And I won't interfere. But, you know, the fact that friendships are fractured doesn't surprise me. I've actually thought a lot about that this summer as I've been writing the story of our neighborhood. Love ebbs and flows, but that doesn't mean it isn't real. Our story has never been perfect. But I still think it's worth telling. And probably your fight with Brian needs to be part of it."

I dusted sand from my hands. "Anyway, enough about that. How's Luka? Is he still in Ukraine with his dad?"

"He comes back in two days," Yolanda replied. "I miss him, but you know it's been a good break. We seem to be at odds with each other more often these days."

"Well, he's a teenager now, right? You'll get through them, but the next few years won't be the easiest. He's a good kid and you've raised him well. You should both come for supper some night after he's back."

I slipped on my sandals and stood up. "I should head back home," I said looking down at Yolanda as she rolled over on her stomach and reached for her book.

"I'm glad you're back," she said, smiling up toward me, one hand shielding her eyes from the sunlight.

"Me too," I said. "I really missed everyone."

There was so much good in the story I was writing—deep friendships forged over many meals together, sacred stories told as we gathered for Writers' Group, honest conversations about faith, doubt, religion, and life. And yet there was so much that was painful and hard. Fran's death, Nicolai's absence, Anna and Ron's move back to the United States. Even before I'd left, things had been shifting. And when I returned, I didn't quite know where to place my feet. The ground felt unsteady.

Just before I returned from sabbatical, Rachel had moved in with her mother and aunties to help her mom recuperate from surgery. Before I'd left Toronto, Rachel and I had agreed she should take a break from hosting Monday night dinners. We both found it exhausting to host without the other being present. Over the years, we'd established a rhythm that served everyone well: Rachel tended to dinner and chatted with friends relaxing at her kitchen counter, while I gave my attention to people seated in the living room, especially anyone who was new to the group.

When Rachel moved back into her apartment, we tried to restart the dinners, but life was more complicated—while we were still committed to loving our neighbors, we'd lived in the same place long enough to develop other commitments as we lived into the inevitable expanding and deepening relationships with friends, not only from our neighborhood, but also from the gym, church, and work.

So, after several stops and starts, we finally agreed the season of Monday night dinners had come to an end. I felt guilty about this at first. *Were we giving up something precious? Something key to loving neighbors?* Yes. Of course we were. *Shouldn't we just try harder?* No, that didn't seem to be the right course.

Eventually, I made my peace with the decision. Loving my neighbors could never be formulaic or dependent on never-ending traditions. I'd come to understand that loving my neighbors was about a posture of preparedness, a readiness to cross a threshold; about being present to people and allowing them be present to me.

But that didn't make the changes I was experiencing any easier. Especially when my friends were not speaking to each other. The rest of us never clearly understood what had caused the rift between Brian and Yolanda, but all of us seemed to sense the futility of mediation. This was between Yolanda and Brian. They'd known each other long enough to work it through if they truly wanted to.

Still, I wasn't quite ready to agree with Yolanda that we were all getting divorced. After all, we'd never been married. We'd been neighbors. And neighbors do come and go. That's the deal. It doesn't mean we don't love each other. It doesn't mean we won't become genuine friends. But often, neighborly love is situational and contextual.

I'd become good friends with many of my neighbors, including Brian and Yolanda. My love for them had no expiration date, and I was grieved their friendship had fractured. I prayed for reconciliation, believing they both had it in them to forgive one another. I knew it was possible because I'd experienced it myself.

About a year into our friendship, Brian had invited seven of us for dinner: me, Ron and Anna, Yolanda, Rachel and, the guests of honor, Rachel's father and stepmother who were visiting from the United States.

We sat around the living room, me in a leather club chair facing the kitchen; Ron, Anna, and Yolanda on the couch; and Rachel on another leather chair in front of a window. Rachel's father and stepmother sat together on a low futon Brian had positioned just below the raised kitchen counter. From their spot, they could see the rest of us but had to turn around to see what Brian was up to at the kitchen counter behind them.

As usual, he was moving quickly around the room, delivering plates of food, refilling glasses. Music, thrumming from speakers attached to Brian's laptop, underscored our lively conversation. Mostly, I paid attention to what people were saying, but gradually I became mesmerized by a series of images scrolling through a digital photo frame on the end of the kitchen counter. Rachel, Anna, Ron, and Yolanda could see them, too, but Brian, ever on the move, was oblivious, as were Rachel's dad and stepmom.

As the images scrolled by, we saw photos of Brian's grandmother, his mom and stepdad, landscapes of favorite places he'd lived. And then the nudes began appearing. Close up images of body parts: muscled legs, sculpted abs. After the close-ups, full body images of Brian and his boyfriend.

All the while, we ate and we talked. The conversation moved from one subject to another with hardly a break. No one mentioned the photos, and I wrestled internally with what to do about the situation, wondering if Brian, who often talked and made jokes about sex, had put them there on purpose. Perhaps he wanted us to see them. But would Brian go that far? I wasn't sure.

But the instant Rachel became aware of the photos, she rose from her seat, brought her plate to the kitchen, and whispered in Brian's ear. She did it unobtrusively, and he immediately turned the photo frame off.

At the time, it never occurred to me that the photos would embarrass Brian. He talked so openly and freely about his sexual experiences, told so many graphic stories. A week later, when Rachel, Brian, and I were having dinner together at her apartment, I even made a joke about it.

"My dad and stepmom really appreciated the invitation to dinner," Rachel said. "I did too. It was really kind of you to have all of us over."

"And, of course, the photo show just added to the whole night," I quipped, expecting Brian to laugh. But he didn't. His face paled. And then, a few minutes later said, "I've got to go. Thanks for dinner, Rachel." And he was gone.

"Maybe I shouldn't have joked about that," I said to Rachel, as we listened to the elevator doors opening and shutting.

"I think you might be right," she replied.

I was raised in a culture where teasing is a conversational norm. We observe people, taking note of their foibles, quirks, and even their failures, storing them all up as fodder for future ribbing. It's a form of indirect affection, not meant to be cruel or mean. The problem is, you never really know how the teasing is being received. More likely than not, the person being teased will laugh it off, or give back as good as he or she gets. Even if they don't think it's funny. Even if the teasing stings.

Brian didn't laugh. He escaped. I was mortified, and I knew I had to do something about my careless words.

Saying I'm sorry is not difficult for me. I've had plenty of practice, thanks in part to my experience as a newspaper reporter and editor. In the early days of my career, a colleague helpfully pointed out to me that, since everything we did would daily be reviewed by thousands of people, we would never be able to hide our errors. The best practice was to own up to mistakes as quickly as possible so we could regain credibility with our readers. We followed a set of simple rules: Admit you got it wrong. Apologize. Try not to make the same mistake twice.

But I am more than just practiced in the art of apology. I also believe deeply in its power. I have asked for and received forgiveness from strangers, friends, and family many times in my life. Each time I have received this gift, my belief in the possibility of reconciliation grows. But even more than these human acts of forgiveness, I believe I am daily forgiven by God for all the things I say and do that cause harm. Forgiveness is central to the life and teachings of Jesus. It's a central theme of the Bible.

Who can discern their own errors? asks the writer of Psalm 22. *Forgive my hidden faults. Keep your servant also from willful sins; may they not rule over me.* This is a prayer I've repeated often.

I knew God would forgive me for hurting Brian. But would Brian?

Before I went to bed that night, I wrote him an email, knowing I wouldn't see him for several days. He was catching a flight to Montreal early the next morning.

> Brian, I have been thinking about how I joked about seeing the photos of you and your boyfriend and I want to apologize. I also want to say I am sorry I didn't let you know they were cycling through your photo frame. I didn't really stop to think you might be embarrassed or caught off guard by the fact I'd seen the photos, because you do tend to joke and talk about sex a lot. But I know joking about something doesn't necessarily mean the person only thinks lightly about it. In fact, sometimes we tend to joke about the things that are particularly vulnerable places, as if the joking helps us put on a protective rind . . .

Brian sent a response within minutes.

> It's not me I am concerned about, but my boyfriend. My photos are in cyberspace, so I have already accepted that someone might see me (albeit someone gay, not straight, not a friend). Maybe it's not smart for me to have done so, but I am very proud of my body and the public is just too conservative. If I don't push boundaries around me, the world will never change. However, where it concerns my boyfriend, certain things are private. With him, I have to think for two.
>
> Sorry to have been so careless. In future—and there will be more mistakes, there always are—please stop me from

doing harm to others ASAP. I need that kind of support, since I can be out of control at times.

I know your heart is in the right place. Yes, I was surprised at how you reacted and discussed it, but then, it's not like you have had to deal with this before.

Thanks for the apology. Sleep well. . . . See you next week. Love, Brian.

A week later, Brian invited me to his apartment so he could show me diagrams of an invention he'd been working on in his spare time. We sat next to each other on the couch, shoulder to shoulder, a large piece of graph paper spread across our laps.

"Here, let me show you the prototype photos," Brian reached down to the floor to pick up his laptop. Then he paused, lightly touched my hand, and gave it a gentle squeeze.

"Don't worry. There are no photos of naked men."

I gave him a sideways glance, a smile playing on my lips; my heart, just inches away from Brian's, beating in quiet equilibrium.

We humans cannot seem to avoid hurting, wounding, or offending one another. We do it regularly, sometimes purposefully, but more because we aren't being attentive. Maybe we're rushing through a conversation and not really listening to the other person or observing body language; maybe we've had too much to drink and our brain is too foggy to interpret anything clearly.

Sometimes the wounds we inflict on each other are unintentional. Sometimes we stab each other on purpose. But to ask forgiveness and to be forgiven, these are not happenstance. These are choices. I was grateful to Brian for forgiving me.

And, I was relieved when Yolanda chose to forgive Brian. It took a long time, nearly a year. But eventually, like when she returned from Kiribati, Yolanda simply walked through the door to Writers' Group one evening and sat down among us, knowing she'd be welcomed back. That night, when the rest of us packed up and left, Yolanda and Brian stayed behind.

I don't know how they got there, but reconciliation was where they ended up.

Early on in my friendship with Yolanda, she told us over dinner one Monday night she did not need forgiveness to carry on with her life. And I suppose in a sense she was right about that. She could carry on. If she lost a relationship, so be it. In the early days of our acquaintance, she always insisted she was fine with that. But as the years added up and we became friends, she also began to acknowledge the powerful gift of true reconciliation—how asking for and receiving forgiveness is worth pursuing. Once, when I asked her what she appreciated about our community of friends, she had this to say: "I am attracted by the fact that people are forgiving. If someone makes a mistake, there seems to be enough trust among us that malice is not suspected."

As I look back on our friendships now, I think Yolanda was right. We annoyed, frustrated, and hurt each other, but rarely on purpose. Choosing to be real with each other meant we exposed our true selves—all the beauty and all the ugliness. Without forgiveness, we'd have been lost.

17

Earnestly Asking

Without prayer, I'd have been out of my depth as I navigated getting to know and falling in love with my neighbors. I prayed—I still pray—for my friends. For as long as I've known them, I've been sending missives upwards on their behalf. I pray in the early mornings as I sit in my living room or on my balcony, watching the day come to life over Lake Ontario. Sometimes at 4 a.m., I awaken with one of my friends on my mind. *Are they in crisis or a place of potential harm?* I ask God to protect them, and, having done all I can do at that moment, sleep usually comes.

Over the years, when I've told my friends I pray for them, their reactions have been mixed but they've never asked me to stop.

"It annoys me sometimes when you pray about me, asking that I would know that I am loved," Rachel once said to me. "It seems so cheesy. Could you not just ask for me to have a solid boyfriend?"

I protested. "I do pray for you to have a solid boyfriend! I don't know why God hasn't answered that prayer yet!"

I also frustrated Brian with my prayers, especially when they were sent up to thwart his efforts to buy street drugs or meet yet another random man through Grindr.

"I was supposed to meet a dealer last night but he didn't show up—were you praying?" Brian would ask me.

"Of course," I'd reply. I wasn't surprised he didn't ask me to cease and desist. God often frustrated him, but Brian did not disbelieve. In fact, he was convinced there was some power in the universe that might be worth seriously engaging, if only he could have a few questions answered first.

"I was talking to God yesterday," Brian told me one day as we walked along the lake. "I was saying, 'you know God, I struggle with you. All the shit I'm seeing in the world, all the atrocities, what's with that?' So God and I are having a conversation, but I'm pretty disappointed in God. If God wants to know me, he's going to have to give me some answers to all the stuff I'm seeing in the news. He's absent, and I don't understand it."

We walked in silence for a few moments, and finally I replied, "I don't have answers for why God doesn't seem to intervene in all the atrocities either. Except, maybe he's given us the tools. I think if we all lived by Jesus' guidelines the world would be a more peaceful place."

"Perhaps," mused Brian, "it's like Mozart—the music lives forever. The message can live forever. But then you throw humanity in the mix and it's all ruined. I know it works for you and Rachel— I can see it. You've found so much peace and so much joy in life. It comes out in the meals you share, the way you want people to experience joy in life too. Can you imagine—I'm not going there— but can you imagine if tomorrow I said I'm tired of living life this way? I'm going to commit to God and Jesus?" Brian laughed. "It ain't never going to happen. I'd check out with drugs first."

We walked on. I didn't have answers for all his arguments, nor did he for mine. But that never got in the way of our friendship. It just made me pray for him more. Over the years, my most frequent prayer for my friends was that they would know they were loved. By me, by others, and, most importantly, by God.

And whether they fully accepted it or not, they at least knew that Rachel and I believed it. Early in their friendship, Rachel had startled Brian one evening when she looked directly at him and declared, "Brian, God loves you."

"That has never occurred to me before," Brian replied.

Many years into our friendship, during the season of Covid-19 when we literally went months without seeing each other, Brian and I frequently communicated by voice texts. Taking a risk one day, I decided to send a voice text that included a prayer to God. I knew I was nervous—while Brian knew I prayed for him, he would never accept my offers to do it when he was present. But that day, I felt compelled to show him, not only tell him, that I interceded for him with God.

"Good morning," I spoke into my phone. "This might be a bit weird for you, and I'm going to give you fair warning so you can choose not to listen. But I'm going to say a prayer for you and give it to you even as I send it up to God. I'm going to do this because I know you don't mind me praying for you, and I want you to hear what I'm going to say."

I took a big breath and launched in: *God, I pray that Brian will somehow sense that he is deeply loved, not only by his friends, but also by the God of the universe.... I believe you gave me my friendship with Brian as a gift, and I pray you will make a way for him to find the peace and purpose and rest in life that he is looking for, that we are all looking for. I pray you will help Brian come alive. I know he talks to you sometimes. I know you hear him.*

Three hours later, I got a panicked voice text from Brian. "Oh my God. I listened to like thirty, sixty seconds and then I stopped as soon as you were hinting we were going to pray together. No, no, no. Listen carefully, I know you care about me ... but I know what I need to do to improve my life. No, no, no!"

Fifteen minutes later, I got a calmer voice text. "Well, obviously God's communicating to me through you. You took me where I did not expect. I have frenetic activity in me. It never stops. I was dual tasking, doing something at my computer. But then I actually stopped what I was doing, looked away from my computer, and closed my eyes and I listened. And I will re-listen. The frenetic nature of me stopped. There was a calm." Brian took a deep breath. "Thank you. That's all I can say. Thank you for caring. Thank you for praying for me. You shocked me. You delighted me."

In my lifetime, I've asked God for many requests that have not been answered in the way I'd hoped—healing for dying friends, restoration for broken marriages, the end of wars. But I've also seen many prayers answered—a miraculous healing of a child, friendships restored, provision for my needs, including the home I'd found when I'd moved to Toronto. On the day I risked letting Brian listen into my conversation with God about him, I was so grateful to hear God's answer through Brian's voice—to know that, at least in that moment, on that day, my friend knew he was loved.

Often my prayers go up to God in the form of questions. *What should I do? What should I say? Why is this so difficult?* Frequently, they are requests. *Help me understand. Help me be less judgmental. Help me grow in wisdom.*

That last request, the one about growing in wisdom, has been part of my life since I had my very first newspaper job, back in the days when I was still a student and only nineteen years old. That summer, I landed a job as the editor of the front section of my hometown newspaper. I was responsible for choosing the news everyone would read each day, for writing the headlines and deciding what appeared above the fold of the paper, and what would go below.

My shift started at 6:30 a.m., and as I walked my daily route to the newspaper office, I'd send up my prayer: *please give me wisdom, please help me know what is the most important news, help me spell everything correctly.* (I was a terrible speller in those days—this might have been the most desperate of my prayers!)

The various dictionary definitions for the word *wisdom* are what you would expect: sound action, decision, insight. But I particularly like this one: the quality of having experience, knowledge, and good judgment. Steve Bell, one of my favorite singer-songwriters, and a sage himself, once described wisdom this way: "Suddenly you know something, not because you are smart, but because it was revealed to you by God."

When I moved to Toronto, I prayed that God would help me understand why he commanded me to love my neighbor. *Why,* I asked, *is this so important? What difference does it make? Why love?*

I don't have all the answers, but, as Steve Bell says, I know something.

After Brian and I had been friends for a few years, I sent him this email:

> I am very thankful to have you in my life. Believe it or not, years ago, I began to ask God to put me in a community of people that would be alive and generous and committed to being with each other. I really believe that prayer has been answered through the group of friends that has sprung up here in this neighborhood. And you are part of the very beginning of that—you and Rachel. I never imagined the circle of friends would be quite like it is, but I wouldn't want it any other way. It is rich and challenging and full of stretching conversations, and a few good laughs, too. (And lots of good wine and food!)

Brian responded:

> Thanks for sharing. Was it you or Rachel who said I am not talking to God enough? It's true, so through you my conversations continue. He sent me here. I know this.

At some point in my forties, I devoted a year or more to reading books about prayer, searching out what the Bible had to say about the practice and putting various kinds of prayer disciplines into my life. For a year, I spent an hour most mornings praying through the Lord's Prayer, stopping at each line and pondering its meaning.

"Our Father which art in heaven, Hallowed be thy name."

You are holy, God. You are above and beyond this earth. What exactly does that mean? Help me to understand holiness . . .

"Thy kingdom come, Thy will be done in earth, as it is in heaven" (Matthew 6:9-10 KJV).

Let me see glimpses of heaven here on earth—more kindness, more love. Help me to see people healed, relationships restored. Help me to see things that are beyond what we humans seem capable of—more generosity, more forgiveness. If your kingdom is about peace and love, show me evidence of that here on earth . . .

And on I would go, working the liturgy out in practical ways, letting it interpret my experiences in life.

When I asked God to help me understand why loving my neighbors was so important to my life, I had no idea how the answer would come. But I believed it would. And it did. The answers are woven all through the story of my life in Toronto and every other place I've lived as well.

When I decided to risk opening the door to strangers who were neighbors, I had no idea they would help me discover so much about myself. One by one, they showed me that loving them, and being loved in return, trumped all my fears about vulnerability and all my need to be in control.

When I asked God why I ought to love my neighbors, he sent them, one by one, to answer the question.

Dancing with Brian

"Want to go nightclubbing with me tonight?" The invitation flashed across my phone as I was setting my coffee mug and purse on my office desk. My thoughts collided. *No. I hate nightclubs. Yes. Brian is inviting me. Why is he inviting me? Where is he inviting me?*

The only other time I'd received such an invitation from Brian was when he organized an evening at a gay strip bar. I was out of town that night, a perfect solution for me. Ever since the Scarborough Fair stripper experience, I've stayed away from clubs where bodies are the main currency.

I texted Rachel. "Did you get an invite from Brian to go nightclubbing?" No. It appeared I was the sole recipient.

I texted Brian back. "Will there be dancing?"

"Yes."

"Where are you thinking of going?"

"The Drake Hotel. 10 p.m. Dinner at my place first, around eight. I'll have you home by midnight."

This was sounding more bearable. Maybe I could even convince Brian to shelve the dancing and just stay at home. I began to imagine a companionable evening that ended with me being back in my own apartment and in bed by eleven o'clock.

I texted him: "Sure, I'll come."

Nightclubs are not my favorite haunts. I much prefer evenings spent in a quiet coffee shop, an elegant restaurant, or, better yet, a friend's living room. I don't enjoy shouting in order to be heard. But I love dancing and an evening with Brian was always time well spent, even if it came at the expense of a Friday evening in bed with a book. The older I get, the more that appeals to me.

"It will be an adventure," I told myself as I changed clothes after work. It was a warm July evening so I chose an aqua blue sleeveless dress and red leather espadrille sandals. They were an inch too high for me but vanity won out. I already knew I'd be out of my comfort zone; I might as well look stylish as I teetered precariously into whatever lay ahead. Besides, I wanted to match Brian's style—I envisioned him wearing his soft, brown leather shoes, glittery gold jeans and a tight white T-shirt. He'd be showing off his six-pack abs (not entirely earned by working out—Brian had paid surgeons thousands of dollars to enhance his body, sculpting it into his own form of currency).

At the Drake, Brian held my hand as we threaded our way across the dance floor, bought drinks, and then found a space to sit on a long banquet seat under the plate glass window overlooking the street. A jovial group of people filled most of the space beside us, anchored by a hefty, slightly drunk man who twisted his attention to Brian and me, friendly and quickly warming up for a flirt.

He's practiced, I thought to myself. *And I'm not interested.*

Brian put his arm around me and sailed comfortably into conversation with our seatmate, making the kind of casual conversation that bores me. I tried not to let it show on my face. Eventually, Brian pulled me to my feet. "Let's dance."

We wandered through several rooms, each with DJs spinning tunes, before we finally worked our way down to the basement where the music suited both our tastes. We weren't looking for a waltz, just fast, fun moves.

Earlier in the evening, as we sat in Brian's living room eating spare ribs and pickled cabbage, I'd asked him how he was doing. It wasn't a superficial question. I knew his mother had died ten days earlier, far away in Germany.

"She's being buried today."

Ah. His invitation was beginning to make sense.

Brian was a good dancer, his feet weaving intricate patterns as he erased one move, redrew another. Several younger guys on the edge of the dance floor were watching him, but Brian took no notice. He'd disappeared inside the beat, eyes shut, head down, hands fluttering against his hips.

"Close your eyes," he leaned toward me and whispered. "Just let the music take you away."

I tried. But I found myself preferring to watch Brian's feet, and the young guys next to us, who also seemed mesmerized by his moves.

Eventually, we took a break and once again Brian grabbed my hand leading me across the floor to a cracked leather couch set against one of the walls. Above the seat, there were dozens of black and white photographs of couples kissing. And above the photos, a neon sign that explained it all: The Kissing Booth.

We sat together on the seat that must have been pulled from a 1960's Pontiac sedan, and placed our drinks and my red leather purse on the small table in front of us. For a while we didn't talk, just leaned comfortably against each other, watching the other dancers: the women in their short black dresses and stilettos, dancing mostly with each other; the men trying to appear nonchalant as they stood against the walls, beers in hand, eyes scanning the dance floor. It reminded me of a ninth grade dance, but with more visible alcohol. I took my cell phone out of my purse and we snapped a few selfies, laughing and clowning around with each other. And then, unexpectedly, Brian turned toward me, leaned closer in, and brushed his lips against mine. It was quick, that kiss, barely a whisper.

And yet, so profound. I received it as a spontaneous thank you from Brian, his way of showing his appreciation for ensuring he wasn't alone on the day his mother was being buried. But more than that, I knew it sealed the truth of our friendship, that in spite of how different we were, we really loved each other.

There is a well-known chapter in the Bible, 1 Corinthians 13, and it's all about love.

> Love is patient,
> Love is kind.
> It does not envy, it does not boast, it is not proud.
> It does not dishonor others, it is not self-seeking, it is not
>   easily angered, it keeps no record of wrongs.
> Love does not delight in evil but rejoices with the truth.
> It always protects,
> Always trusts,
> Always hopes,
> Always perseveres.
> Love never fails.

These poetic lines are most often read at weddings, words of advice for two people committing the rest of their lives to each other. But I think they apply equally to neighbors, to people we encounter in life, sometimes for a moment or two, sometimes for a few months, a year, perhaps even a lifetime.

Neighborhoods come in all shapes and sizes. There are quiet suburbs where people exit their cars by way of garages, never using their front doors. Every front lawn looks perfect. No kids play there, preferring the predictable safety of fenced back yards. There are inner city streets lined with row houses, where people might at least say hello as they mount their veranda steps. There are small towns and villages where traditional neighborliness is preserved by community dinners at the local arena. I happen to live in a vertical neighborhood, with hundreds of people (and their dogs) next to me, below me, on top of me. We can't help but be aware of each other, in the hallways, the parking garage, the elevators, the bus stop. But that doesn't mean we actually see each other.

Some of these neighborhoods are more inclined to neighborliness than others. But none of them are inclined to love. Love is a choice we—the people who make up neighborhoods—make.

Would Jesus, if telling a Good Samaritan story today, place an isolated neighbor at the center of the parable? What might he want to awaken in us by telling a story of someone whose wounds are as real as that injured man on the lonely road, but less visible? The point of the parable would be the same.

Love God, and love your neighbor as yourself. It's quite the statement, this rule of life that is to be applied to oneself, to others, and to God. Each has a role to play in seeding, strengthening, and sustaining relationships among us.

What does it mean, I asked God, to love my neighbor? And why the word *love*?

Pay attention. Notice. Engage. Welcome. Open your door. Invite people in. Accept their invitations in return. Give time. Risk being yourself. Share food. Share stories. Laugh. Debate. Apologize. Forgive. Cry. Celebrate. These are the threads that, when tossed to and fro between neighbors, become a tapestry of love.

Toss your thread out. Catch the one coming your way. Do it now, when the person is right in front of you. Don't wait.

Come for Dinner

I was tired and rumpled, having just flown the red-eye from
Vancouver to Toronto. I grabbed an airport taxi, eager to get
home and climb into my own bed for a long sleep. I'd been away
for several weeks and was hauling a hefty suitcase and carrying a
knapsack full of books, my computer, and a camera. Waving hello
to the concierge in the foyer of my building, I headed for the elevator. It was 7:30 a.m.

Inside the elevator, I pushed the button for the fifteenth floor
and leaned against the wall. I closed my eyes as I made the rapid
trip skywards. The doors opened and before I could shake myself
awake, I heard a gleeful shout.

"You're back! I've missed you so much! I'm so glad to see you!"
Raffi threw her arms around me as I stepped out of the elevator.

"Wow, what a welcome," I said, trying not to let Raffi see my
tiredness. "I'm glad to see you too!"

Raffi and her parents were new neighbors who had been living
next door to me for a couple of years. Within a month of their arrival, fourteen-year-old Raffi had found her way into our lives and
then invited her parents along too. Yolanda was the first person to
meet Raffi, literally colliding with her as she left my apartment one

evening. Raffi was on her way to the recycling room, her arms full of boxes and bags.

"Here, let me help you," Yolanda offered. And by the time they'd reached the main floor, Raffi had been invited to Monday night dinners. Soon she introduced us to her parents, Breno and Nina, and before long, they were all adopted into our circle of friends.

A year after we'd met them, Breno, Nina, and Raffi hosted a dinner in their apartment, inviting Rachel, Yolanda, me, and Angie, another neighbor new to our building. The invitation came by email:

Dear friends,

It has been a little more than one year since we moved to the area. We would like to celebrate and thank you for the love and friendship we have received from the very first day. Having you as close neighbors is the best part of living in this area. Please come dine with us and spend a couple of hours in our place.

Best, Breno

I loved having Breno, Nina, and Raffi as neighbors. We shared a balcony, with just a glass partition between us. If I stood on my tiptoes, I could peer over the top. We were close enough to exchange more than cups of coffee over our balcony railings—we passed many things between us: my homegrown tomatoes and sprigs of mint, their special Brazilian desserts and, for all of us, time—lots of time.

Raffi released me from her hug and reached for my suitcase. "Here, let me carry that," she said. I didn't argue. I handed it to her, and we walked down the hallway together.

Acknowledgments

*S*hortly after moving to Toronto, I stopped writing a newspaper column, the place my published writing had resided for nearly a decade. It was a heartbreaking decision made easier when my wise friend Janet Buckingham suggested that, for a season, I should focus on living into community, not writing about it. I'm glad I listened.

Many people have been great encouragers to me in the five years it's taken to write this book. Deborah Carr, you read the first draft, asked tough questions, and said, "Keep going." Rebekah Rotert, you never stopped saying, "Write this story." Ian and Naomi Elliot, time and time again you welcomed me into a lovely space to write and wrestle and wander. Alan and Glynis MacGibbon, without your generosity, I wouldn't have moved into this particular neighborhood.

I'm grateful for the Humber College creative writing program where I honed early versions of this book under the guidance of incredible mentors. Anne Michaels, thank you for telling me I had a voice and MG Vassanji, thank you for telling me I was confusing and needed to be more straightforward about my faith.

Mom, you and Dad laid the groundwork in my life for faith, hospitality, and courage. Thank you.

Ethan McCarthy, you are a gentle and intelligent editor. To the whole team at InterVarsity Press, thank you for loving writers as well as books.

To my neighbors, thank you, from the deepest part of my heart. I wish I could honor you individually here, but we agreed I would change your names and some details about your lives. Using interviews, my journals, and emails, I've done my best to be faithful to our shared story. I know your perspective would be different than mine, which makes me even more grateful for the trust and grace you've extended to me. This book couldn't have come to life without you.

Notes

FOREWORD

[1]Zygmunt Bauman, *Postmodern Ethics* (Oxford: Blackwell, 1993), 240.

[2]Ann Morisy, *Bothered and Bewildered* (London: Continuum, 2009), xi.

[3]Tim Soerens, *Everywhere You Look* (Downers Grove, IL: InterVarsity Press, 2020), 44.

2. CHASING A QUESTION

[1]Michael Frost, *Incarnate: The Body of Christ in an Age of Disengagement* (Downers Grove, IL: InterVarsity Press, 2014), 167.

[2]Frost, *Incarnate: The Body of Christ in an Age of Disengagement*, 73.

5. OPENING MY DOOR

[1]Scot McKnight, *The Jesus Creed: Loving God, Loving Others* (Brewster, MA: Paraclete Press, 2017), 54.

[2]McKnight, *Jesus Creed*, 148.

7. PAIN AND PLEASURE

[1]Leon Morris, *Testaments of Love: A Study of Love in the Bible* (Grand Rapids, MI: Eerdmans, 1981), 41.

12. JOY AND SORROW

[1]Jake Meador, *In Search of the Common Good: Christian Fidelity in a Fractured World* (Downers Grove, IL: InterVarsity Press, 2019), 44.

15. BEYOND ACQUAINTANCES

[1]William Somerset Maugham, *The Mood and Sixpence* (London: George H. Doran Company, 1919), 265.